BILL T

CLICK SAND

HOW ONLINE MARKETING
WILL DESTROY YOUR BUSINESS

(AND THE UNLIKELY SECRET TO SAVING IT)

IDEAPRESS
PUBLISHING

Published in the United States by Ideapress Publishing.

IDEAPRESS PUBLISHING | WWW.IDEAPRESSPUBLISHING.COM

All trademarks are the property of their respective companies.

ISBN: 978-1-940858-43-2 (Print)

Original Cover Designer: Alban Fischer

PROUDLY PRINTED IN THE UNITED STATES OF AMERICA
BY SELBY MARKETING ASSOCIATES

SPECIAL SALES

Ideapress Books are available at a special discount for bulk purchases for sales promotions and premiums, or for use in corporate training programs. Special editions, including personalized covers, custom forewords, corporate imprints and bonus content are also available. For more details, email info@ideapresspublishing.com.

For Kim,
my muse for 35 years.

CONTENTS

PROLOGUE

....

CAUGHT IN THE TRAP

"But the Emperor has nothing at all on!"
~ from "The Emperor's New Clothes,"
by Hans Christian Andersen (1805–1875)

Quicksand was a staple of movies and TV shows in the 1960s. For audiences, it was suspenseful and scary. For production studios, it was a special effect that was simple and inexpensive. Just dig a pit, fill it with oatmeal, add some shredded wine corks on top and voilà, your hero or heroine is suddenly in mortal danger.

There were many shows that incorporated quicksand into their plots. As a child of the '60s and '70s, though, I most remember it from the classic TV series *Gilligan's Island*. The show was a slapstick comedy, but hidden among the hijinks were interesting ideas for a young mind to ponder. I still remember being captivated by the episode where the castaways laid out a giant SOS with logs that they planned to light on fire as a space capsule passed overhead in orbit. The SOS would alert the passing astronauts that there were people stranded down below. Gilligan botched the plan by accidentally setting himself on fire and moving the logs to spell "SOL" as he ran around frantically trying to douse the flames. Being that *Sol* was the name of one of the astronauts circling high above, the sign was interpreted as a good-luck message to Sol and his crew. So the castaways were thwarted once again in their attempt to be rescued.

The idea that someone could lay out a message on the ground that would be seen by astronauts in space, however, captured my imagination. Anything related to space was magical in those days, when space travel was still very new and the thought that I could do something that would communicate with a real astronaut was fascinating to me. I recall lying awake at night thinking about whether I could build such a sign in our backyard. What message would I spell out? Would it have to be made out of logs or could I use some other material for the letters? How would I know if the astronauts actually saw it? Eventually, though, my mind became occupied with other ideas and I never built my message to space.

In addition to astronauts (and headhunters and amazing contraptions built from bamboo), quicksand was a staple of *Gilligan's Island* stories. There was an episode where the Skipper fell into quicksand and Gilligan tried to save him. Gilligan made a mess of things, of course, and the Skipper ended up having to save himself. In another episode, Thurston Howell III pretended to be dead by placing his hat on top of quicksand to make the others think he'd fallen in and met his demise. And then there was the episode with Lord Beasley Waterford.

Lord Waterford was a British authority on butterflies who arrived on the island searching for a tropical butterfly called the Pussycat Swallowtail. During his hunt through the jungle, he unwittingly walked right into quicksand as he was fixated on one of his desired specimens. In the scene, Lord Waterford continued to be so captivated by the beauty of the magical creature in front of him that he had no idea he was sinking toward his demise. Luckily for him, the Howells were nearby and rushed to rescue him.

While astronauts captured my imagination as a child, it's Lord Beasley Waterford's quicksand experience that resonates with me today as a business owner and marketer. Millions of business owners are sinking into a trap that could kill their companies, yet they don't even realize it. Instead, they are focused on the pursuit of a mythical creature described to them by the online marketing industry: a prequalified, ready-to-buy customer that will magically appear in their inbox.

While quicksand in *Gilligan's Island* is supposed to represent a natural phenomenon, *clicksand* is a trap that has been built by the pitchmen of online marketing: digital platform companies like Google and Facebook, software providers like HubSpot and Constant Contact, and even smaller agencies and marketing consultants in every town across America. The common goal of these pitchmen is to sell ever more to the companies that trustingly follow their advice even if it damages or destroys those companies in the process.

In the following pages, I'll show how the clicksand trap distracts businesses with activity instead of progress. It offers an enticing promise that with just the right recipe of keywords, email subject lines, or social media posts, customers as rare and magical as the

Pussycat Swallowtail will appear. It's a ploy that has been explicitly designed to lure unsuspecting businesses ever deeper into the trap toward their death.

Fortunately, more and more business owners are starting to suspect that they are in the clicksand trap and the feelings those business owners are experiencing tend to follow a similar pattern.

THE PERSPECTIVE OF THE (BUSINESS)MAN ON THE STREET

Over the past couple of years, my conversations with business owners who have been unhappy with the results of their online marketing efforts have all contained a common thread. Whether they are in manufacturing, professional services, technology, or some other field, these business owners express similar feelings:

- **Frustration.** They're disappointed that the online marketing techniques that are all the rage these days aren't performing as promised for their company. A lot of marketing activity and energy are being invested, but somehow it's not translating into revenue.

- **Confusion.** They can't understand why online marketing seems to be working for everyone but them. And when they try to get answers, the response from online marketers is a bunch of technobabble and mathematical minutia that leads to even more expenditures—financial, emotional, and time—but still with no results.

- **Fear.** They've heard over and over that online marketing is permanently changing the way forward-thinking companies grow their business, and that anyone who doesn't keep up will be swept aside. So even though their online marketing program isn't working for them, business owners don't want to abandon it . . . just in case!

- **Dissonance.** They also have a nagging sense that many of the techniques they are using in their online marketing campaigns just don't feel right. Things feel artificial, forced, and insincere—especially when compared to how their company built its success up until that point. In some cases, these business owners have been pushed to become social media celebrities, even though their own (and the company's) personality skews toward low-key. Or a business owner will find their online marketing strategy necessitates creating content and advertisements that aren't authentic to what the business really believes. Frequently, the business owner feels as though they're being encouraged to focus on a high volume of shallow, transient interactions when the company has, historically, built its business around fewer yet deeper relationships.

- **Isolation.** Lastly, these business owners have been thinking they're the only ones in the world questioning the value of online marketing. They've seen stories of resounding success in trade magazines and at conferences from others in their industry. They've been barraged by vendors and consultants who claim that online marketing is foolproof. Even their own employees have pressed for online marketing in order to make the company more "with it" and "on the cutting edge." In the face of this constant stream of breathless enthusiasm for online marketing, it feels as if everyone else sees something that they, the business owner, are missing. They're afraid to share their misgivings about online marketing for fear of appearing out of touch as a leader.

Take heart: you are not alone (you're definitely not the only business owner potentially trapped in clicksand) and you're not out of touch. Many other business owners share your feelings (I encounter them every day!) and I assure you that you are *more* in touch with what is really important to the success of your business than the online marketing pitchmen trying to convince you to change the way you do business.

BUT WHY A BOOK AT ALL?

Author and public speaker Simon Sinek has popularized the concept of "Start with Why" in business circles in recent years. He explains that people don't care about *what* you do—they care about *why* you do it. It's a concept I've always loved and when my partners and I started our company, Civilis Marketing, in 2010 we spent considerable time thinking about why the world needed another marketing firm. This book was born out of that introspection.

Every day, businesses are being taken advantage of by some of my peers in the marketing world—marketers that are more concerned with making a buck than they are with helping their clients. Many of those disillusioned clients come to Civilis Marketing to get their marketing campaigns back on a productive track. When my team explored the "whys" that get us fired up about marketing, we realized that one of the things we all feel passionate about is helping business owners avoid the clicksand trap—whether those businesses work with us or not. Our team is energized to shine a light on the pitchmen and alert business owners to the dangers of signing on with these charlatans.

There are probably *millions* of businesses that have already fallen for the ideas of the online marketing pitchmen. In recognition of the formidable pressures that business owners face, *Clicksand* is my effort to reach all of the business owners my firm can't work with directly—to help those who've already been convinced by a pitchman to choose a marketing path that could ruin their business and to aid those who have not yet fallen into the trap to avoid it altogether.

HOW THIS BOOK IS ORGANIZED

Clicksand covers three topics related to what is happening in the online marketing world today:

1. **Compelling: How the Pitch Works.** Snake oil is a term that's loaded with emotion. In Part 1 you'll find out how the sales techniques used by online marketers today follow the same approach used by snake oil salesmen of the 1800s and how businesses who fall for the pitch are damaged…and in some cases, completely destroyed.

2. **Compounding: Why the Pitch Is So Successful.** Effective snake oil sales pitches capitalize on other things that are happening in the world, giving them a boost in attention or credibility they wouldn't otherwise have. Part 2 looks at how the pitchmen of online marketing are benefitting from several societal and scientific trends that help their pitch work particularly well. (In fact, it works so well that most of the people giving the pitch really do earnestly believe it themselves!)

3. **Correcting: How to Avoid or Get Out of the Trap.**
Part 3 walks you through a framework and provides a set of
resources that you as a business owner can use to critically
examine *what really drives your business growth and success.*
This knowledge will allow you to rebuild your sales and
marketing approach in a way that's both authentic and
effective—which will give you the confidence to decide
to use or not use online marketing tools as you see fit.
Plus, you'll be armed with the self-assurance to ignore the
pitchmen who will try to convince you that your business
is "missing out" or "falling behind."

WHAT'S OLD IS NEW AGAIN

Online marketing tools and techniques are typically viewed as
a radical departure from the way sales and marketing were done
before the advent of the Internet. But most of what is happening
today in online marketing—from how business owners are feeling
about their campaigns to the way the tools and techniques are being
hyped by proponents—is not new at all. There are many lessons
from the past that can help us to view online marketing in its proper
historical context.

You'll see how today's online marketing mania mirrors events
in the settling of the American West, relates to the theories used
by casinos to encourage gamblers to bet more, and even ties to the
first cave paintings by prehistoric man.

Our journey begins 125 years ago with the gentleman who
made "snake oil" a term for the ages.

PART 1

....

COMPELLING

Breaking down the components of a snake oil sales pitch and showing how today's online marketing pitchmen follow the same age-old recipe.

1

THE RECIPE FOR SNAKE OIL

"If more of us valued food and cheer and song
above hoarded gold, it would be a merrier world."

~ J.R.R. Tolkien (1892-1973), author of
The Lord of the Rings trilogy

In the summer of 1893 at the Chicago World's Fair, Clark
Stanley, a thirty-eight-year-old Texan, set up a booth to demonstrate
a liniment rub he claimed would cure such wide-ranging maladies
as sciatica, insect bites (animal and reptile bites, too!), sore throat,
toothaches, bruises, and even frostbite.

As fairgoers looked on in awe, he would reach into a bag of
rattlesnakes, pull one out, slit it lengthwise, and plunge it into
boiling water. The oils from the snake would float to the top of the
water and Stanley would skim them off and use them to mix up a
batch of his liniment right before their eyes.

The demonstration was so enthralling that visitors started buying it on the spot, making Clark Stanley's liniment a huge hit.

Stanley went on to build a company with production facilities in Massachusetts and Rhode Island, running ads in newspapers across the country promoting the benefits of his Snake Oil Liniment. For the next twenty-three years, customers continued to buy the product, apparently without noticing that it was manufactured in a part of the country where there were no rattlesnakes whatsoever.

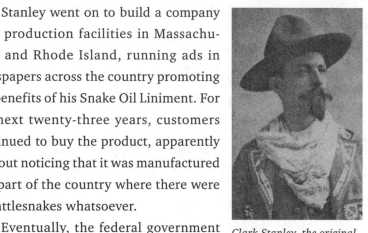

Clark Stanley, the original snake oil salesman

Eventually, the federal government passed the Pure Food and Drug Act of 1906 in an effort to safeguard the public from products that were misleading or unsafe. Stanley's Snake Oil was tested and found to have five ingredients: mineral oil, red pepper, turpentine, camphor, and a very small amount of fatty oil, which was presumed to be beef fat. Not a drop of rattlesnake oil. Clark Stanley was fined $20 (about $400 in today's money) for false labeling and inflated claims. Thus, the term "snake oil" began to become synonymous with exaggerated or misleading products—a derogatory label still used more than a hundred years later.

But is that negative connotation still warranted? There was no snake oil in Stanley's liniment, so the label definitely was misleading—but was it so misleading that it should be the eternal poster child for fraudulent marketing?

THE MORE THINGS CHANGE...

When it comes to misleading labelling, things aren't much different today.

The next time you're in a grocery store, grab a jar of McCormick's Bac'n Pieces and read the ingredients. You'll see that there's no bacon included—in fact, there's no meat of any kind in the salad topper. There is, however, soy flour, canola oil, salt, caramel color, maltodextrin (a thickener or filler), natural and artificial flavors, lactic acid, yeast extract, disodium inosinate and disodium guanylate (flavor enhancers), and red food dye. The apostrophe in *Bac'n* is apparently the secret. Maybe if Clark Stanley had labelled his liniment as "Sn'ke Oil," he might have avoided his infamy.

Or check out a bag of Wise Onion Rings. The snack contains absolutely no onions at all. Look closely, though, and you will see the word "flavored" wedged in between the words "Onion" and "Rings" on the bag.

Apparently, "Snake Oil–*Style* Liniment" would have been enough for Clark Stanley to avoid trouble with his product name—and today's marketers have learned how to sidestep Stanley's mistake with subtle changes to their product labels.

Stanley went further than choosing a misleading product name, however, by adding claims that his liniment could cure a surprisingly long list of maladies. Indeed, marketers are doing the same thing today.

One of my favorite examples is the Wonderful Company's line of pomegranate juice and blended-juice beverages. A few years back, a federal

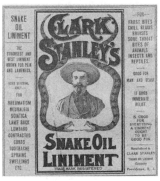

An original ad for Stanley's Snake Oil

lawsuit found that the company was making deceptive disease prevention and treatment claims. The court admonished the company for implying that its pomegranate juice products could treat, prevent, or reduce the risk of a long list of conditions, such as heart disease and erectile dysfunction. Imagine if Clark Stanley had known how big the market was for sexual performance enhancers!

While misleading labels and claims are as common today as they were in Clark Stanley's day, modern marketers are better at avoiding legal trouble related to their cure-all products and services—and online marketing pitchmen are some of the worst offenders.

How exactly do they do it and why do their tactics work so well? Deconstructing how Stanley's liniment became such a success over a century ago reveals the techniques still used by the snake oil salesmen of online marketing today.

THE THREE Ps

Clark Stanley didn't just invent his snake oil liniment out of thin air. His product and its extensive claims for cures originated from a real product: a traditional folk remedy that came to America with Chinese laborers in the 1800s. The Chinese immigrants came by the thousands to work on back-breaking projects, such as the transcontinental railroad. They brought an ointment made from the oil of the Chinese water snake, which is rich in omega-3 fatty acids that help reduce inflammation. After a long, hard day at work the Chinese workers would rub the oil on their aching limbs and backs. Eventually, they began sharing the oil with some of their American coworkers, who claimed it really did help with problems like arthritis and bursitis, which were common among manual laborers.

There were no scientific medical experiments or clinical trials to prove that the Chinese snake oil had any documentable curative powers, but word of the relief it provided spread anecdotally. In this era before FDA requirements and approvals, customer testimonials were the best advertising and good enough to spread the word and create demand.

As more and more people heard that Chinese snake oil had helped them, demand for the ointment increased. Eventually, Clark Stanley created his own oil product to capitalize on the reputation of that original folk remedy.

Stanley realized that the recipe for making snake oil wasn't about what was in the bottle at all. The *real* ingredients necessary to make snake oil were external societal factors, which can be summed up in three *P*s:

- **Pain.** First, there must be a problem that people are anxious—or even desperate—to solve. In the 1800s, medical maladies like arthritis were crippling diseases with no treatment or cure. Sufferers would try just about anything to get relief. This created a pent-up demand for any product that could capture the attention of potential customers.

- **Promise.** Rumors of anecdotal successes are necessary to spark the imagination of pain sufferers. In Clark Stanley's case, this came from the word-of-mouth testimonials of people who had tried the original Chinese snake oil rub. Customers who had benefited from that product helped spread the word about snake oil in general. It didn't matter whether it actually worked or not. Just the rumor (the promise) that it might work was enough to kick Stanley's company into high gear.

- **Plausibility.** An explanation of how or why a product works also helps. The explanation, though, doesn't even have to make logical sense. Stanley's snake-boiling routine at the World's Fair caused crowds to go wild for his product. He didn't prove that the liniment would actually cure arthritis pain. His dramatic demonstration simply showed how new and innovative his product was. It was something no one had seen before and that was enough to have people step up with their money to buy a bottle.

That's the recipe: pain, promise, and plausibility. It's one that's tried and true: what worked so well for Clark Stanley in the 1800s still works for the pitchmen of the online marketing world today. Today's pitch starts with tapping into the pain that many contemporary business owners experience.

2

"Many a small thing has been made large by the right kind of advertising."

~ Mark Twain (1835–1910), American author and humorist

Retail titan John Wanamaker was one of the most innovative businessmen ever, building some of the first big department stores in the world in the 1800s. Wanamaker was the innovator of many ideas that are commonplace today, including the money-back guarantee and the evolution of "fixed pricing," where the price of an item was clearly marked and nonnegotiable. He literally invented the price tag.

Wanamaker was also a sales pioneer who recognized the power of marketing and advertising earlier than his contemporaries. In 1879, his department store was the first ever to purchase a full-page newspaper ad, and his was the first business in any industry to hire a full-time copywriter. During the six years that copywriter John Emory Powers worked for Wanamaker department stores writing six ads per week, the company's sales doubled from $4 million to $8 million.

By any measure, John Wanamaker had marketing success that most business owners can only dream about. But he was still frustrated with the inexact nature of marketing, supposedly proclaiming, "Half the money I spend on advertising is wasted; the trouble is I don't know which half." With all of his success, even the inventor of many modern marketing approaches had a problem that all business owners still face today: not having a reliable process for predictably growing a business.

John Wanamaker, marketing innovator and philosopher

Unfortunately, many businesses these days aren't even doing as well as John Wanamaker did by getting it half right. Over a century later, when today's business owners are asked about their biggest challenges, difficulty growing revenue and market share remains a top concern.[1]

It's not that sales and revenues aren't growing for many companies. The pain that business owners feel is rooted in not being in command of whether they grow or not. John Wanamaker doubled his company's revenues and still felt as if he only halfway understood how he'd done it. Modern business owners—whether their bottom line is growing or not—often feel exactly the same way.

---

1 https://www.entrepreneur.com/article/242432, http://www.waspbarcode.com/small-business-report

While successful business owners are able to manage most aspects of their company, from customer satisfaction to quality control to cash flow, many can't generate sales projections for the next year and define how they will hit the target. This inability to predict—and manage—sales growth creates two types of stress for business owners:

- **Workplace Stress**. So many decisions, from staffing to investing in infrastructure to managing credit, are based on whether and how much the business will grow in the future. Without the ability to accurately predict future revenue, all of those decisions become significantly more difficult and risky.

- **Personal Stress**. Surveys of entrepreneurs[2] consistently show that freedom, autonomy, and self-determination are important motivations for owning a business. Inability to accurately predict and manage sales is a dilemma that bleeds into the business owner's personal life.

This personal pain can make a business owner just as susceptible to an online marketing pitchman offering a cure-all as any arthritis sufferer who saw Clark Stanley's rattlesnake boiling demonstration.

EXACERBATING FACTORS

There are two additional factors—one external and one internal—that can magnify the pain level of business owners who

---

2 http://www.inc.com/ilya-pozin/10-best-reasons-to-be-entrepreneur.html, https://www.gov.uk/government/uploads/system/uploads/attachment_data/file/408432/bis-15-132-understanding-motivations-for-entrepreneurship.pdf, http://www.rediff.com/money/2005/apr/19spec.htm

are feeling as if they don't have command of their marketing and sales results.

All companies are faced with a shortage of available sales talent, resulting in high-level sales positions remaining unfilled. If doubling revenue requires doubling the size of a sales staff, it's just about an impossibility in today's job market. When an idea comes along that promises "leads and sales without needing additional salespeople" it will inevitably sound appealing.

Additionally, many companies do not have a clear, documented process for how marketing and sales lead to revenues in their own business. In many cases, sales have occurred organically through long-term relationships, the reputation of the owner, or even referrals from happy customers. Companies that have grown to $5 million or even $50 million in revenue often don't have a comprehensive understanding of exactly how they got to where they are today.

Without a detailed understanding of all the events and elements that contributed to their past success, business owners will lack a clear edit point for what kind of approach is right for the future. As a result, they will be vulnerable to exploitation by unscrupulous online marketing pitchmen who come armed with distant stories of mythical successes.

3

PROMISE

"I offer my opponents a bargain: if they will stop telling lies about us,
I will stop telling the truth about them."

~ Adlai Stevenson II (1900–1965), American lawyer,
politician, and diplomat

Anecdotal tales of success are the fuel source that initiates demand for all types of snake oil. Repeated stories hailing a cure (for back pain, backyard weeds, wrinkles, poor sales, etc.) feed the hopes of pain sufferers who are desperate for a solution. Clark Stanley capitalized on the rumors of relief provided by the mysterious rub used by Chinese laborers in the 1890s, and similar second- and thirdhand stories lay the groundwork for pitchmen in online marketing today.

It seems that all business owners know a story of someone in their world who is *supposedly* succeeding with online marketing.

Most commonly, a business owner will see the online marketing efforts of a competitive firm and believe that effort, in and of itself, to be proof that the competitor is *successfully* using online marketing. The hopeful business owner will talk about the great-looking email newsletter they got from the competitor, the perception that the competitor seems to be ranking high in Google searches, or that they have noticed more LinkedIn posts from the competitor lately. The business owner has made the assumption that simply seeing evidence of the competitor's marketing efforts is proof that those efforts are producing sales for that competitor.

Urban legends of online marketing successes spring from other sources, too. Sometimes, business owners show me a magazine or web article that highlights how another company in their industry has embraced online marketing.

Other times, they'll return from a conference where they were mesmerized by a speaker promising that online marketing is going to completely revolutionize how all business is done in the future.

I've even had business owners tell me they heard about an online marketing program from an acquaintance at their kid's soccer game or while attending a backyard barbecue.

Whatever the source, these urban legends of supposed online marketing successes are sufficiently intriguing to pique the interest of business owners. The chance that there *might* be a cure for the sales and marketing pain they feel is enough to get business owners to investigate further by reaching out to an online marketing firm or attending an event about online marketing to learn more. That's when they get hit with one of the standard promise tools of the online marketing industry: the case study.

YOUR RESULTS WILL VARY

Clark Stanley, the original snake oil pitchman, became the standard-bearer for sales conmen by making misleading claims that his Snake Oil Liniment would cure all manner of ills, from toothaches to insect bites. Customers fell for Stanley's assertions without any scientific evidence or objective research showing that the claims were true.

Today, as consumers and business owners, we are more sophisticated than people in the 1800s, and we routinely require some proof of success before we buy in to a new idea claiming to help alleviate a pain we are suffering from. However, that doesn't mean we're not still susceptible to conmen. Just like toothache sufferers from Clark Stanley's era, anyone experiencing pain secretly *hopes* that a new idea really will be the cure they've been wishing for. No matter how skeptical we like to think we are, we're hardwired to want to believe.

Today's online marketing pitchmen know that they have to make their misleading claims come across like evidence and research even when they're not. They do this with several case study techniques:

- **Redirection.** Online marketing pitchmen have a problem: Often, the tools and techniques they're selling cannot really fix the problem the potential client actually has. In order to make the sale anyway, the pitchmen use a "diagnosis-style" case study to reframe the product story to make it seem as if their snake oil is the perfect solution. For instance, if a business needs more potential revenue in its sales pipeline, an online marketing salesman might reframe that problem by showing that the business's website has a low volume of traffic. Of course, a thin new business pipeline could be caused by myriad other issues. But by confidently "diagnosing" the problem as a web traffic issue, the pitchman is able to transform the problem into something he can address with the slick online tool he's offering. The case study ends by triumphantly announcing that the business's web traffic jumped spectacularly—conveniently omitting performance information about the original sales pipeline problem.

- **Implication.** Online marketing pitchmen love to tout their existing clients' marketing metrics—making it seem as though those metrics equate to business success. The promise of becoming an "industry leader" is a common tactic. They will show that a client has become a leader in its industry by presenting marketing metrics such as number of Twitter followers, volume of speaking engagements, or level of Google search traffic. They imply that those marketing metrics are indications of business success and that the client is "leading" its industry in all aspects of its business, not just in marketing metrics.

- **Correlation.** Frequently, online marketing pitchmen present successful business performance data of their clients alongside marketing data, and they make it appear as if the marketing data caused the business success. In this approach, "sales growth of 22 percent" is listed along with "email newsletter subscribers up 53 percent," suggesting that those things are related. Most of the time, there is no evidence that one led to the other.

- **The Self-Case Study**. One other technique that marketing pitchmen frequently use is to display their own success at selling snake oil as proof that their clients are also successful.

They use their clients' logos or marketing industry awards they've won to make the case that they must be helping clients succeed. My firm had a business owner come to us while still working with an online marketing company that had touted themselves as platinum-level resellers of the HubSpot software tool. The owner thought that the platinum reseller status proved that the marketing firm were experts he could rely on, but he came to realize that it only meant that they had been very successful in selling a lot of snake oil to other business owners just like him.

With anecdotes and careful presentation, the pitchmen of online marketing are able to create a very compelling display of supposed proof that is just as effective as Clark Stanley's. But the pitchmen of today take it further than Stanley ever did with one final sinister twist.

FOMO

Psychologists call it "Fear of Missing Out" (FoMO). It's the anxiety that we all feel when there is a limited quantity or a limited window of time to get involved in something that's appealing or necessary. Limited-time-only Black Friday sales drive frantic shopper behavior with this fear. In life-threatening situations, stampedes can occur, kicked off by FoMO, if there is a perception that there aren't enough seats in the lifeboats.

Online marketing pitchmen use FoMO by proclaiming that the world is permanently changing and any business that doesn't embrace the new online marketing paradigm will be swept aside. They usually say it with a helpful and positive tone, acting as though they are trying to encourage businesses to capitalize on the fantastic opportunities that are available in this new marketing era.

But underneath, the meaning is clear: in addition to promising to cure the pain that business owners feel, the snake oil salesmen of online marketing are subtly promising death to anyone who doesn't get on board.

It's a threat that drives business owners to try to learn what this "online marketing phenomenon" is all about. And the online marketing industry is ready with a captivating presentation of plausibility.

4

PLAUSIBILITY

"It doesn't have to make sense, it just has to sound like it does."
~ Elmore Leonard (1925–2013), American author

As Clark Stanley proved with his spectacular presentation at the 1893 World's Fair, snake oil salesmen don't have to demonstrate how their product actually works—or, for that matter, that it even works at all. Certainly, it was dramatic for Stanley to boil rattlesnakes and mix a batch of his liniment from the remains right on the spot, but that flashy spectacle didn't explain how or why his concoction would have any effect on sore joints. So why did people line up to buy his product? Because they *wanted* to believe.

In the recipe for selling snake oil, plausibility appears after pain and promise for good reason. Potential customers start with a pain that they are desperate to get relief from. They then hear the promise of a new potential cure, which raises their hope that their suffering might finally end. This hope paves the way for the snake oil salesman's plausibility case. At that point, potential customers don't need to see proof of a new remedy's effectiveness; the solution only needs to seem *new and different*.

Pain sufferers of all types, whether they have a physical ailment or a business problem, tend to be well informed on all of the potential solutions that already exist. They've tried everything else that has come along with no success. Potential customers for a snake oil salesman, therefore, only have to be convinced of one thing: that this new cure-all is not like all the other things they've tried before that didn't work.

Clark Stanley simply had to show that his liniment was different than all the other products people had tried previously for their arthritis pain. His snake boiling demonstration accomplished that objective dramatically and effectively.

Today's online marketing pitchmen have a demonstration that works just as well.

BOILED LOGIC

It starts with energy—lots of energy. Online marketing pitchmen are some of the most enthusiastic and animated people you will ever meet. They may not be boiling rattlesnakes like Clark Stanley did, but they definitely attempt to bring the room to a boil with their energy during presentations. Some use a high-energy style, some have a kitschy or funny gimmick, and others make it memorable with a pop of colorful language. Without fail, they all speak super fast.

No matter their personal style, all pitchmen explain their exuberance with the premise that they have so much wonderful information to share that they are bursting at the seams. I don't think I've ever seen an online marketer, whether in a big convention presentation or one-on-one in a conference room, who didn't start with some variation of, "I'll go really quickly because there is so much great material here that we won't be able to touch on everything and I want to give you as much as possible!" Some speakers I know in the online marketing world use PowerPoint presentations and will flip to a new slide every three to five seconds. That's more than *six hundred* slides in a fifty-minute keynote speech. The material is propelled at attendees like a jet of water from a firehose, a pace that conveniently eliminates any opportunity for critical questioning or thoughtful exploration by attendees.

Once the breakneck speed has been established, there are three kinds of presentation techniques online marketing pitchmen tend to use:

- **Linear Human Behavior Assumptions.** Without fail, online marketers present an unrealistically simplified view of how human relationships work. They reduce complex, emotional creatures to a diagram that shows a clean, inevitable progression of actions where A leads to B, then C, and so on. It might be "customers search on Google, see your ad, click on it, and go to your landing page;" or "you post a funny picture, they click 'like' on your post, then their friends see it;" or one of myriad other possibilities. This simplified view of the way people act is based on the way that the computerized tools that online marketers push work, not based on the way humans actually behave. In real life, relationships never follow a predictable series of steps. There are side trips and reverses and a million variables that can't be preprogrammed. Confidently ripping through a slide every three to five seconds, though, the online marketing pitchmen make it seem like they have it all figured out.

- **Technobabble.** Online marketing pitches are inevitably peppered with a dizzying array of tools and technical terms. First, there are dozens of different sites and platforms, including Google, YouTube, Facebook, WordPress, HubSpot, Constant Contact, and many more. Every site and platform has a multitude of features, techniques, and analytics: ranking algorithms, retargeting, A/B testing, boosted posts, click-through rate, reach, tracking pixels, and so on. To the uninitiated, it looks and sounds like *Star Trek* science fiction discussions of warp-field inversions and Heisenberg compensators. And even though most of the terms are about as valuable as the imaginary technology in *Trek,* this language is still enough to impress business owners hoping for something different.

- **No Money Down.** The final act of the online marketing pitch is the revelation that a business can try it for almost nothing—or literally for nothing in many cases. Facebook pages are free; you can do the work yourself to try to get your website to show up higher in Google's page rankings; and posting thought-leadership opinion pieces to LinkedIn costs nothing. Even things that do cost money are positioned as small investments (that are bound to yield huge returns, of course!). Online advertising campaigns start at about $50. A professional email newsletter program will only cost $20 a month. The online marketing pitchmen make it seem as if thousands or even millions of dollars in business can be yours with just a few inexpensive clicks of a mouse. Of course, it never works out that way. But the low cost to start makes it seem as though there is little risk.

Just like arthritis and toothache sufferers at the World's Fair more than a century ago, today many suffering and hopeful business owners buy into the pitch of online marketing and step forward to embrace the cure-all.

Some quickly realize that it isn't the magical solution that was promised. But far too many stick with it even when it isn't working, causing damage to their businesses—especially if their success has historically been built on long-term, personal relationships.

5

THE DAMAGE

"Without reflection, we go blindly on our way, creating more unintended consequences, and failing to achieve anything useful."

~ Margaret Wheatley (b. 1944), American writer and consultant

There are two types of damage that happen to businesses that have unquestioningly followed the advice of online marketing pitchmen: the damage that unscrupulous online marketers do to their clients directly, and the damage that business owners do to themselves (and the employees, families, and other stakeholders who rely on the business for their livelihood).

Let's start with the first kind: where the pitchmen knowingly take advantage of their unsuspecting clients. In his book, *Disrupted,* Dan Lyons shared an insider's view of how disingenuous HubSpot, the online marketing software company, was as it pretended to be "changing the world" in the early 2010s. In reality though, as Lyons illustrated, the HubSpot image and mystique was just a front for a boiler-room sales operation designed to sell as much software as possible to drive up the revenue of the company in preparation for its IPO.[3] The scheme worked for what Lyons called the "amoral" founders of HubSpot—to the tune of $880 million in 2014.

For the businesses who were sold a bill of goods by the HubSpot sales machine, however, life wasn't so rosy. Current and former HubSpot clients make up a significant portion of the businesses who come to my firm for help when things don't work out as promised by the HubSpot reps and partner agencies. The owners of HubSpot got their money, though, and that was likely all they really cared about.

Other firms are even more blatant than HubSpot—simply taking customers (and value) away from their subscribers from right under their noses. A great example of this is the Vetstreet.com service from global veterinary service conglomerate Henry Schein, Inc.

One of the "helpful" offerings that Vetstreet sells to local veterinarians across the country is a social media content service. For about $250 a month, Vetstreet creates syndicated, interesting, pet-focused stories that can be automatically posted to a local vet's Facebook page. On the surface, this service appears to help overworked vets keep their Facebook pages active and engaging with a constant stream of new content—something they always have trouble doing consistently given the craziness of their daily schedules. Vetstreet has been able to sell this service to many local veterinary practices across the country in the last few years, positioning its services as a way to be supportive of the great work that veterinarians do for the pets we all love so much.

---

3 Dan Lyons, *Disrupted: My Misadventure in the Start-Up Bubble* (New York: Hachette Books, 2016).

What Vetstreet is really doing, though, is siphoning off the pet-owning customers of those local veterinarians for Vetstreet's own benefit. Every one of those interesting Facebook posts that veterinarians are paying Vetstreet to post for them are just teasers for longer articles. To read the article, the pet owners on the local veterinarian's Facebook page have to click on the post, which then takes them to the longer article on Vetstreet's own website. Once the pet owner arrives at Vetstreet.com, Vetstreet then works to develop its own relationship with the pet owner—frequently cutting the local vet out of all future interactions.

Vetstreet pretends that the Facebook article posting service they sell to veterinarians is designed to help the local vet build more visibility and business, but in reality, the whole program appears to be designed to allow Vetstreet to strip mine the customers from local vets across the country into a huge, valuable national database of pet owners that Vetstreet can then make money from. At last count, the service had siphoned off a loyal audience of more than three million such customers from local vets across the country—all while getting vets to each pay Vetstreet $250 a month.

Stories of similarly unscrupulous services abound in the online marketing world thanks to the daunting number of tools, options, and features available—as well as the breakneck pace of change in the industry. Most business owners can't keep up with every nuance and subtlety of the marketing industry to know whether an attractive-sounding pitch from a HubSpot or Vetstreet is a good idea or scam.

But the damage from the online marketing pitchmen doesn't just stop with rip-off offerings directly from the pitchmen themselves. It often goes much further—business owners are harming their *own* businesses by following the advice of the pitchmen.

STOP HITTING YOURSELF

Business owners who buy into the sales pitch of online marketers run the risk of damaging their own businesses in three different ways.

First, a push toward volume and efficiency can inhibit or even eliminate the ability of the business to nurture important individual relationships. For businesses where success hinges on long-term personal relationships, future growth potential can be seriously harmed by some of the types of marketing tools and programs being pushed.

Second, the high-volume techniques typically sold by the pitchmen create a mindset where businesses view potential customers through a negative lens instead of a positive one. Rather than seeing new relationships as opportunities, new relationships are viewed initially with a focus on filtering and disqualification. Starting out of the gate with a cynical perspective reduces the chances of establishing rapport in new relationships.

Finally, the opportunity cost of focusing time and money on the wrong marketing and sales approach while ignoring other approaches that have worked well in the past can set businesses back significantly.

FIRST, DO NO HARM

Will Rogers, the famous actor and columnist, once said, "It takes a lifetime to build a good reputation, but you can lose it in a minute." It's much the same with relationships. They are built like a tower, brick by brick, over a series of interactions that begin simply and grow in complexity and depth over time. But the whole thing can come tumbling down in an instant if rapport is broken.

Unfortunately, many businesses are convinced by online

marketing pitchmen to use techniques that are all but guaranteed to break rapport with the very people the business would like to get to know better—starting with the most fallacious technique of all: marketing automation.

Broadly speaking, marketing automation (also known, hilariously in my opinion, as "marketing intelligence") is a set of predetermined messages and actions that will supposedly initiate and nurture relationships with potential customers from first contact all the way to (or close to) purchase.

That a computer could be interacting with potential customers in the background while the business owner works on other things, alerting them when the sale is ready, sounds wonderful. This is the impossible dream that online marketing pitchmen sell. But a simple real-life scenario can easily show that not only does this tactic not work, it can seriously damage a business's reputation and eliminate any future potential for the business in the process.

I, ROBOT

Imagine walking into the opening cocktail reception at a convention in your industry. Assume there are several people at the reception that you'd like to talk to—prospects you'd love to have as customers. Now assume that, just like marketing automation, you are going to preplan the first three sentences you will say to all of those people when you run into them—sentences designed to move them toward buying from you. You might want to start with a light quip—you don't want to come on too strong—about the winter weather in Chicago that delayed flights of some people who were coming to this convention. Then you could pivot a bit and mention that you're glad your flight wasn't delayed, because there is a session that relates to your company's product early tomorrow morning you want to attend. Finally, you'll be ready with a nice elevator pitch when the person you're talking to asks what your company sells. You'll have your opening sentences all planned out to deftly move your prospect from first contact to sales lead:

1. "I heard that a few folks were delayed in Chicago with that snowy weather they're having there."

2. "I'm just glad my flight wasn't delayed because I'm really looking forward to the session tomorrow morning on the applications of phaser technology in the next century."

3. "I'm at PhaserTech and we provide world-class consulting solutions to the turbo phaser industry and always give new customers a 20 percent discount on their first order."

It looks great on paper—just like a marketing automation sequence—so you head over to start a conversation with one of the prospects you want to meet (we'll call him "John"), confident that you are on the path to sales success. In reality, you're hurtling toward disaster.

THE BEST-LAID PLANS

Of course, you can't predict what John's response will be when you deliver your first sentences about the snowstorm in Chicago. He might mention that he was lucky to get rerouted through Minneapolis so he avoided the delays. He might respond that he knows all about snowstorms in Chicago because he lived there for ten years in the 1990s. He might say that his daughter is stuck in Chicago trying to get to a job interview she has in LA. Heck, it might be so loud at the reception that John might even say, "Sorry, what?" In fact, the possible number and variety of responses from John are infinite and definitely not predictable. Chances are slim that your comeback about "being glad you didn't get delayed because you're looking forward to the session tomorrow morning" will be an appropriate response to whatever John says.

If you do get lucky and your response isn't totally inappropriate, though, things will only get worse. If John doesn't ask either why you're looking forward to the session tomorrow morning or ask what business you're in, your sentence about what your company does will be so wildly off topic that John will think you're either mentally unbalanced or way too pushy.

Within sixty seconds, you'll have ruined any chance of building rapport with John—now or in the future. And the longer you keep going with preplanned, robotic sentences, the worse it will get. It would have been better to have never talked to John at all than to try to use the "automation" approach to building rapport with him.

Of course, any experienced businessperson would know better than to rigidly spout a series of preplanned sentences in such a conversation regardless of what the other person responded with. It's preposterous and disingenuous.

Despite this obvious absurdity, businesses are convinced to do this very thing every day by online marketing pitchmen selling the "automation" of relationships. Sound bad? It gets worse.

ME, MYSELF, AND I

The other problem with a preplanned series of communications is that, since you don't know what John will say when you talk to him, you can't preplan anything to say about *him*.

Even if, in some miraculous twist of fate, your preplanned sentences actually make sense related to John's response, everything you say will still be about yourself. If you're able to avoid coming across as unbalanced or pushy, you will *definitely* come across as self-centered, which will also ruin any chance you have to build an authentic relationship with John.

All experienced salespeople know that the key to building rapport with another person is to be *interested in them*—not to talk about yourself. If you're in the office of a prospective customer and you see a fly fishing photo on the wall, you spend time asking about fly fishing. Diploma from Notre Dame? Ask how the new quarterback is working out. And for certain, you will remember whatever is discussed this time for follow-up next time you interact with that prospect.

Marketing automation, with its rigid, predetermined messaging approach requires that all prospective customer interactions follow the same inflexible path and it can't treat each prospective customer as an individual. It can't talk about fly fishing with Prospect A and the new Notre Dame quarterback with Prospect B. Marketing automation cannot build and nurture individual relationships. It can't listen to and care about the person on the other end of the message. It can't talk (or better yet, ask) about what the prospective customer cares about. That level of sensitivity still requires a human.

For businesses where success hinges on building and nurturing authentic, long-term, individual relationships, following the automated approach of the online marketing pitchmen can be very damaging.

This brings us to the second type of damage that businesses can suffer from by falling for the vision presented by online marketing pitchmen: a vision that actually turns businesses against their prospective customers with an adversarial mindset.

ASK LEWIS ABOUT IT

Elias Lewis (more commonly known as E. St. Elmo Lewis) was an early pioneer in many of the methods that are now standard practice in the advertising world. One of the earliest inductees into the Advertising Hall of Fame, he founded a successful early advertising agency called, literally, The Advertiser's Agency, in 1896 and gained notoriety in the advertising world with his slogan "Ask Lewis About It." He achieved national recognition as an outstanding lecturer, writer, teacher, and leader in advertising.

In addition to doing work for his own clients, Lewis advocated industry-wide on the theories and best practices of advertising. His most notable idea, put forth in 1898, was the concept of the customer journey. Lewis proposed that potential customers went through a series of mental stages—akin to stepping stones—on their way from first hearing about a product or service to eventually purchasing it. Lewis described those stages as Awareness, Interest, Desire, and Action, typically shortened to the acronym AIDA. Lewis further suggested that the purpose of advertising was to encourage and assist customers in moving from one stage in the purchasing journey to the next.

It's an idea that has stood the test of time, and the AIDA concept is still used extensively in mass consumer advertising (think of Super Bowl ads as the ultimate attempt at getting the Awareness of as many people as possible).

But the AIDA concept has been altered by online marketing pitchmen into a version that's different than what Lewis intended—a version that harms many unsuspecting businesses in the process.

HEADS VERSUS HANDS

The tools of online marketing are, in general, good at recording actions taken by the people who use them, such as opening an email, clicking on a Google ad, or visiting a particular website page. As a result, online marketing pitchmen have hijacked Lewis's *mental* stages and turned them into *action* stages, or "conversions." They convince business owners that these conversions (opens, visits, clicks, downloads, inquiries, etc.) are good indicators of where potential customers are in their journey toward purchasing.

At first glance, it may not seem like this migration to a conversion model is particularly troublesome. Online marketing pitchmen, in fact, position it as beneficial, promising that for the first time a business can have objective behavioral data to indicate exactly where potential customers are along the path to purchase. But the practical reality is that the alteration of the original Lewis model into a conversion model has very negative consequences.

REDUCTIVE VERSUS PRODUCTIVE

Online marketing pitchmen typically show their conversion model in the shape of a funnel. The idea is that buckets of prospective customers are dumped into the top of the funnel and filtered and qualified by their conversion behaviors as they move down through the funnel toward becoming a customer. This view of the customer journey as a filtering process is an inherently negative one—a reductive process akin to separating wheat from chaff. The original model of E. St. Elmo Lewis was a *productive* process designed to woo and encourage potential customers (Lewis explained that the role of advertising was, "to catch the eye of the reader, to inform him, to make a customer of him"), not seek ways to eliminate them.

Businesses that structure their sales and marketing programs around the conversion model pitched by online marketers, though, are beginning every new relationship with a negative opinion of prospects by default. That's hardly the way to form a productive relationship. As a result, business owners using this model often become better at listing the reasons that a particular prospect is *not* attractive than they are at finding reasons to invest in the relationship. In effect, they end up running marketing programs that are designed to find reasons to *not* build relationships with prospects. It's no wonder that such programs don't result in sales.

AFTER YOU, I INSIST

Another negative implication of the conversion model that online marketing pitchmen promote is that prospects often must be the ones to act first in order to move the relationships forward. The fact that the decisions and responses of the business are based on the actions that prospects have taken (clicks, views, opens, downloads, inquiries, etc.) means that, in order for the relationships to progress, prospects have to, in effect, prove themselves "worthy" of a response. On the surface, it might seem like a prudent move to only invest time and resources in prospects who have shown behaviors that indicate a good level of interest. That logic might make sense from a dispassionate, analytical perspective, but we're talking about human relationships here. From a *relationship* standpoint, this approach requires that potential customers invest in the relationship before the business will reciprocate. This is yet another rapport-breaking approach that will result in fewer potential relationships being developed.

SACRIFICING THE FUTURE

Ultimately, the worst damage I see in businesses that have fallen for the online marketing pitch is more than just having a marketing program that isn't succeeding. It's that business owners often buy into the dream so much that they modify their company in a futile effort to chase the mirage put forth by the pitchmen. There are three common changes that businesses make that can damage the long-term ability of the business to survive:

- **Abandoning What Really Does Work.** Techniques that have succeeded in the past, like in-person visits, hand-written thank-you notes, or even just a handshake and a smile—things that probably built the business to where it is today—are frequently tossed aside as old-fashioned and outdated. But it's not just old techniques that are abandoned; it's frequently existing relationships, too. I've sat with business owners who are unhappy with their online marketing sales results and asked them where their best current customers came from. Invariably, those customers are the result of long-term relationships that go back many years. When I ask how long it's been since the business owner (or anyone on their team) did anything to nurture those obviously valuable relationships, I often hear that they've been ignored while the business has been focused on the exciting new idea of online marketing. This means that not only has the online marketing effort failed, it's possible that momentum in relationships that really have paid off in the past has been lost, too.

- **Missing Larger Opportunities.** Many of the most attractive potential customers for a business don't (or won't) fit into the conversion approach sold by online marketing pitchmen. I often use the axiom "whales don't click" in my business to remind clients of this truth. Customers who might spend a million dollars with you are just not clicking on Google ads; they're not submitting inquiries through a website form; and they're not signing up to receive promotional email newsletters. The biggest, most attractive customers are working with people and businesses who have taken the time to invest in getting to know them. Focusing only on the prospects who *will* click or open or download causes businesses to miss many of the largest and most lucrative opportunities.

- **Lesser Offerings.** Missing out on the largest opportunities leads to another pitfall for businesses under the spell of online marketing pitchmen. Frequently, those businesses start chasing smaller and smaller prospects by creating smaller offerings: assessments, test drives, introductory offers, "light" versions of their product, and so on. Smaller offerings, in and of themselves, are not a problem if there is a real need that they satisfy in the marketplace. But we frequently see businesses creating these kinds of offerings as a response to low-quality or casual sales inquiries received through programs sold by online marketing pitchmen. These businesses end up chasing inferior quality sales prospects by creating inferior versions of their products and services. Not only is the time and energy that's put into developing the inferior offerings a distraction, there is the risk that the business could be less attractive to higher-quality customers due to the perception that the business is focused on smaller customers.

HOW IS ALL OF THIS POSSIBLE?

In the face of all of the damage that can be caused by following the advice of the online marketing pitchmen, the logical questions are: why are so many business owners falling for the pitch? How is it that a business owner will forsake their proven, relationship-based revenue generation model for a model that isn't capable of building and nurturing relationships? Why do they stick with it when it isn't working? And why would a business owner go so far as to change the way they do business to try to match the false expectations promised by the online marketing pitchmen?

It turns out that there are several societal forces in play today that are making the online marketing pitch more appealing now than it might have otherwise been in any other era. The pitchmen just happened to hit on a message that's right for the times, and they're getting help from some unexpected places.

PART 2

....

COMPOUNDING

Historical and societal factors are magnifying
the allure of online marketing and giving the
pitchmen an unfair advantage.

6

THE INFRASTRUCTURE OF IRRITATION

"If I have seen further than others, it is by
standing upon the shoulders of giants."

~ Sir Isaac Newton (1643–1727), English mathematician,
astronomer, and physicist

Few people today would guess that the world's first unsolicited
sales messages (the ancestor of today's "spam") went out to unsuspecting potential customers more than 135 years ago.

Aaron Ward was a traveling salesman based in Chicago in the
late 1860s. He sold dry goods and general merchandise to retailers
and customers in small towns all over the Midwest. Over time, he
began to believe that there could be a new way to get better-quality
products at lower prices to rural Americans. With the advent of
railroads and a reliable postal system, he wanted to cut out the
middlemen and sell directly to customers, who would order by mail

and pick up their goods at the nearest train station.

Ward, however, faced serious obstacles. The general reaction from his friends and business acquaintances was that the idea was lunacy. And when he started acquiring inventory in preparation for launch, he lost it all in the Great Chicago Fire of 1871.

Still, he persevered, and in August of 1872 he formed a company based on the middle name that most people knew him by: Montgomery. The first Montgomery Ward & Company "catalog" was actually just a single sheet of paper advertising a handful of products that was mailed to rural homes.

Aaron Montgomery Ward

Montgomery Ward's vision paid off, and by 1883 the single sheet had grown into the "Wish Book," a catalog of more than two hundred pages with ten thousand items for sale. By the early 1900s, over three million people were being sent books weighing more than four pounds apiece. Competitors came along as well, with Sears, Roebuck and Company debuting its catalog in the 1890s.

Not everyone was happy with the new direct mail selling approach. Small-town retailers considered the mail-order companies a threat and sometimes publicly burned the catalogs. Many potential customers found a use for the catalogs in their outhouses—to the point where the large

The forerunner of today's "spam"

supply of free "tear-out sheets" from both the Sears and Ward catalogs actually hindered the early development of the toilet paper industry.

Still, direct mail continued to grow in volume and sophistication over the twentieth century as the postal service introduced free rural delivery and catalog companies began tracking which towns and neighborhoods were more likely to purchase different products. It became clear that "junk mail," as it was called by those who disliked it, was here to stay.

THE NUISANCE FACTOR

In the 1970s, the level of intrusion into the lives of Americans jumped to a new level with the advent of toll-free and high-capacity telephone lines. Now there was no need to wait for the long turnaround reply time of a catalog. Companies could simply dial the phone to sell to individual consumers directly and immediately as they desired.

With telemarketing, unsolicited sales messages moved from irritation to interruption. Mail-order catalogs waited passively in the mailbox until retrieved and read by the recipient. A telemarketing call, however, required the recipient to answer at the whim of the company making the call. Calling companies quickly realized that they could most easily reach people in the early evening around the dinner hour, which simultaneously increased the response rates of the calls and the irritation level among the consumers being called. There was a tension between companies wanting to make more calls to drive sales and consumers wanting to receive fewer calls. This tension was something I was able to witness myself from inside the telemarketing world.

In the early 1990s, I worked at a polling firm that called people across America to get their opinions on various topics. Having a room full of human telephone interviewers was a big operating expense, so there was always financial pressure to find ways to reduce costs in that area. The most glaring area of inefficiency was "downtime." Interviewers doing anything other than having a conversation with a survey participant was like throwing money into the trash.

In the early days, interviewers would dial numbers to find someone new to talk with as soon as they finished with an interview. This time spent dialing wasn't only considered downtime, it was also a morale killer because often the interviewers would have to dial number after number until they reached someone, or worse, when they finally did reach someone, they'd get chewed out by that person for calling in the middle of dinner. The interviewers often spent more time trying to find someone to interview than they did actually doing interviews, which made the job less efficient for the company and less enjoyable for the interviewers.

The promise of an answer to both the downtime and the morale problems came to the telemarketing industry in the form of computerized dialers. The dialers could take a big list of phone numbers and automatically dial the numbers as needed. The computer would work in the background, dialing numbers while interviewers were talking to a survey participant. In that way, the drudgery work of having the interviewers dial number after number and the downtime between calls would be eliminated, because the computerized dialer could have a new survey participant ready to go for each interviewer as soon as they finished a call.

It sounded great in theory, but in real life it wasn't quite that simple. There was a built-in trade-off between efficiency (for the company) and irritation (for the would-be survey participants). The most efficient (and therefore most profitable) approach was to have the dialer dialing lots of numbers in the background, ensuring that whenever an interviewer finished a call, there would be another survey participant ready to go immediately.

Constantly dialing numbers in the background, however, meant that some people would answer their phone when there was no interviewer ready to conduct an interview. The dialer, therefore, would have to hang up on them. This, understandably, irritated the people who were hung up on, increasing their general hatred of telemarketers. More efficiency and profit in the short term (by making more calls in the background) would cause damage to the reputation of the entire telemarketing industry in the long term.

In fact, there was an actual "nuisance factor" setting on the computer dialing equipment that could be turned up or down to make more or fewer calls in the background—with more calls equating to more "nuisance" to the people the computer would have to hang up on if no interviewer was ready to take the call when the person answered. There was always a spirited debate within the company about increasing efficiency by treating people more rudely or being less efficient and treating people more politely. I have to admit that, unfortunately, the efficiency camp won the argument more often than not and the nuisance factor was turned up.

With the upsurge of unsolicited telemarketing phone calls, Americans began to fight back against the marketing and sales messages they didn't want to receive. It was one thing to have some extra pieces of mail sitting in your mailbox, but it was something else again to have your dinner or favorite TV show interrupted by a sales call. As a result, the first filtering and opt-out tools for communications began to proliferate to help consumers and businesses control the flow of unwanted intrusions, including caller ID, unlisted numbers, call blocking, and, eventually, the National Do Not Call Registry.

Behind the scenes, however, the government and universities had unwittingly developed a system that would raise annoying, unwanted marketing and sales messages to a previously unimaginable level.

YOUR TAX DOLLARS AT WORK

One of the most interesting historical trends in marketing is how unsolicited marketing and sales messages tend to piggyback on public infrastructure networks that are initially designed to try to help Americans stay connected to each other.

Montgomery Ward's innovative catalog business was only possible because it could capitalize on the U.S. Postal Service that had come into its own in the 1800s. Ward could have never been profitable if he'd had to build the infrastructure himself to communicate to and receive orders from millions of rural homes in America. The rise of the public postal communications network reduced the cost of communicating to the point where he could cheaply send four-pound catalogs to people who had never requested them—just in case they *might* want to buy something.

Likewise, telemarketing was only possible once there was a national telephone network in place that reached virtually all Americans. With the infrastructure in place and deregulation lowering prices, the cost of reaching Americans with telemarketing became affordable enough that companies could begin calling people with the same "just in case" approach that Montgomery Ward had pioneered by mail.

Of course, postal and telephone-based marketing were only the warm-up acts for an unfathomable deluge of unwanted marketing messages that have proliferated on the largest communications network in history: the Internet. Like the postal and telephone networks that preceded it, the Internet has provided a platform for marketers to send unwanted messages—mostly via email—to potential customers, but at much greater volume: almost twenty billion messages per day.

The sheer quantity of unwanted messages in the world today is certainly unprecedented, but it's not just the volume that's problematic. It's also the fact that a significant percentage of the unwanted emails sent to us are deceptive and dangerous.

It's almost nostalgic to look back on the days when unwanted messages were just a catalog in your mailbox or a phone call trying to sell life insurance. Today, unwanted messages are often misleading and some are criminal attacks that contain malicious code or viruses.

Day in and day out, we are all witness to the worst ethics humanity has to offer in our email inboxes. And in the context of so much blatantly negative behavior, slipping just a bit into the gray areas ourselves doesn't seem as bad as it might otherwise. For many business owners, the bar has been lowered for what are considered to be acceptable marketing practices.

IT'S ALL RELATIVE

I find that just about everyone has their own personal strategy for deciding how fast to drive on the freeway. Some drive way over the limit and use technology like radar detectors to avoid getting caught. Others stick strictly to the posted speed limit.

My own strategy is eight-over: I usually drive just eight miles over the speed limit. There is no science behind it. It only feels like seventy-three in a sixty-five-mile-per-hour zone isn't fast enough to be dangerous or get pulled over.

When I'm on a road with no other traffic, I set the cruise control at eight-over and never give it a second thought. I've noticed, though, that my eight-over approach can change when other cars are on the road.

In the background, my brain seems to keep track of an ongoing "passed/got passed" ratio as I drive. Since I'm going a bit over the speed limit, I always expect to pass a certain percentage of the other cars on the road with me. I also expect a few maniacs to pass me, but if I find myself passing more cars than usual, I start to feel like something is wrong and I'll back off a bit—even if there is no evidence of anything actually *being* wrong. It just doesn't feel right to be zooming past too many other cars and I also start to worry that everyone else knows something I don't.

Likewise, if I'm getting passed more than usual, I'll have a desire to bump up my speed beyond my usual eight-over to get back to my passed/got passed ratio comfort zone. The speed that feels "right" to me is affected by how fast others around me are driving.

Psychologists and philosophers would use the terms "contextualism," "situationism," and "relativism" when discussing how I adjust my speed based on what other drivers are doing around me. Many studies have shown that the way others around us are acting is a powerful influencer of our own individual behavior.

Moral and ethical standards can change based on the relative situation we find ourselves in and what other people around us are doing. This effect is happening today in online marketing. Business owners have become accustomed to a world where they're bombarded with unwanted, unethical, and even illegal marketing messages. As a result, their own moral and ethical standards have unconsciously slipped, especially with regard to the use of email.

BUT OUR MESSAGES ARE VALUABLE

It's such a common practice today that few businesspeople give it a second thought: a business card gets exchanged in a conversation at a convention and then gets added to an email newsletter distribution list—even though the person never explicitly asked to receive the newsletter.

Merriam-Webster defines "spam" as "unsolicited, usually commercial email sent to a large number of addresses." Sending an email newsletter repeatedly to someone who didn't ask for it, therefore, *is* spamming. We've all just become so numb to the idea of sending and receiving unsolicited messages that it feels okay compared to the scams and viruses sent by the *really* bad guys.

Another example that happens frequently is the purchase of "opt-in" email lists from list companies to add contacts to an email marketing campaign. The list company claims that all of the people on their lists have explicitly chosen to receive email marketing communications. I've never met anyone who knowingly asked to have their email address sold to an unlimited number of companies they've never heard of before so they could receive spam email messages. I know that I've never knowingly asked to receive spam, but I get hundreds of those messages each week nonetheless. We all do. To purchase and send unsolicited email messages to such a list requires a slip into the gray areas of marketing ethics that seem okay compared to the worst lapses we're all bombarded with every day.

The most common way that businesses and marketers justify pushing the limits of professionalism and courtesy with online marketing is by focusing on the value of the content they are sending to the prospects who didn't ask for it. The logic goes like this: "They didn't specifically say they wanted to get our newsletter, but we put articles in there that are informative and useful, so we're providing a value to them—plus they can always opt out if they don't want it."

On the surface, this seems like a good argument that justifies sending unsolicited communications. In reality, I've never met a business manager who felt that the messages they were sending out weren't valuable to recipients, no matter how blatantly self-serving their messages were. They think that everyone else's unsolicited emails are tacky, desperate sales pitches, but their own messages are valuable offers, tips, and ideas that benefit the recipients.

Generally, as business owners, we've all become increasingly okay letting our standards slip, because we're constantly barraged by behavior worse than our own.

YOU'RE RUNNING A FEVER

The noise and irritation we all experience in today's world is bad enough, but unfortunately it doesn't stop there. We're also being negatively affected by a dangerous and powerful fever that has infected the business world in recent years.

7

GOLD FEVER

"We already have–thanks to technology, development, skills, the efficiency of our work–enough resources to satisfy all human needs. But we don't have enough resources, and we are unlikely ever to have, to satisfy human greed."

~ Zygmunt Bauman (1925–2017),
Polish sociologist and social theorist

Malaria was still endemic to the wetlands of the southern and central United States in the mid-1800s, and in 1844, it struck James Marshall, a recent migrant from New Jersey who had begun cattle farming along the Missouri River. On the advice of his doctor, Marshall decided to leave Missouri to see if a different climate might improve his health. In the spring of 1845, he headed west on a wagon train journey that would eventually change the lives of millions of people all over the world and redraw the map of North America, yet it would leave Marshall himself to die alone and penniless.

By 1845, Marshall had settled in California, which was still part of Mexico at that time. He'd acquired some land and began trying his hand at cattle farming again. But in 1846, war broke out between the United States and Mexico and Marshall left for a time to serve in the conflict. When Marshall returned to his California farm after the war, he found that all of his cattle had either wandered off or been stolen, so he was forced to take a job as a carpenter. He took over the building of a new sawmill for his friend and neighbor John Sutter.

James Marshall

On January 24, 1848, Marshall was helping build Sutter's Mill when he found gold in the nearby American River, east of Sacramento. The discovery kicked off the California Gold Rush.

WHAT A RUSH

The last half of the nineteenth century was the era of the gold prospector, with more than fifty different gold rushes taking place around the world between 1848 and 1899. The granddaddy of them all, though, was the one that prompted the worldwide search for gold: the California Gold Rush.

More than three hundred thousand people flocked to California to try to strike it rich, causing unforeseen changes in California and all over the world. San Francisco grew from a village of about 200 people in 1846 to over 150,000 residents by 1870. The immense distances between the new land of riches and the existing population centers of the United States spurred development of coast-to-coast telegraph and mail communications as well as transportation infrastructure. Regular steamship services were developed to provide more reliable transportation between the Atlantic and Pacific around the southern tip of South America. Within a few years, transcontinental railroads cut cross-country travel times from weeks or months to just a few days.

The California Gold Rush also dramatically changed the political map of North America. California was the first state to enter the Union that wasn't contiguous with the rest of the nation when it was granted statehood. The expansion of U.S. territory that had been marching slowly westward a state at a time took a giant leap across the continent to definitively make the United States a two-ocean, continent-spanning nation.

The effects of the California Gold Rush were felt all over the world, too. The money generated from the gold fields spurred growth in international trade all around the Pacific Basin. The economies of places as far afield as Hawaii (then known as the Sandwich Islands), Chile, and Australia were energized by the sharp increase in California's demand for food and manufactured goods.

WHAT IS A RUSH?

In economic terms, a rush is a race to grab something of significant value that's free or almost free for the taking but limited in availability. This creates a sense of urgency and a flurry, or "rush," of activity.

Gold rushes are the most well-known type of rush. Rushes can occur in any situation, however, where there is something to be gained by being both early and lucky to get something of significant value at little or no cost.

One of the more interesting rushes in history began at high noon on April 12, 1889. That morning, fifty thousand people gathered along the border of the Oklahoma territory in a line that stretched out over hundreds of miles. Beginning at twelve o'clock (with a few people jumping the gun to go sooner, leading to today's Oklahoma "Sooner" moniker), everyone raced in to claim a parcel of land out of two million acres being given away by the U.S. government.

This Oklahoma Land Rush is probably the most accurately named "rush" of all time since it took place pretty much in a single day. Not only did many people rush in to grab the free land that

Photograph of the start of the Oklahoma Land Rush

was available, others rushed in to serve those involved in the rush, with entire cities appearing on the plains within hours. Oklahoma City and Guthrie each went from open prairie at noon to towns of ten thousand residents with streets laid out, lots staked off, and the beginnings of municipal government institutions by sundown on that first day.

Rushes take place all the time on smaller (but no less competitive) scales, too. Across America every year in the wee hours of the morning on Black Friday, consumers jostle and race to get the best limited-availability deals at retailers as soon as the doors open.

Today, a new rush is taking place before our very eyes in the world of online software and technology.

THE NEW GOLD FIELDS

On February 4, 2004, a group of college students launched an Internet-based social media and networking service out of their dorm room at Harvard University. Most of the code for the site had been written in the previous thirty days by one of the students, sophomore Mark Zuckerberg.

The site, eventually called Facebook, was an instant success and quickly grew in users and value. Just over eight years later, the company went public, at a value of more than $100 billion.

We take stories like this in stride in the crazy, technology-driven world we live in today. It seems commonplace to us that a multibillion-dollar company can be dreamed up and brought to life by a few college students practically overnight, because we've heard story after story of high-flying Internet startups that explode onto the scene and sell for billions. But if we look at this in an historical context, the scale of these rags-to-riches stories are truly remarkable.

According to U.S. Geological Survey estimates, approximately twelve million ounces of gold were retrieved during the first five years of the California Gold Rush, with another eleven million ounces recovered through larger hydraulic mining techniques in the years after that. Combined, that amount of gold would be equivalent to about $30 billion today.

This means that Facebook, just one of a multitude of successful digital and social media companies that have appeared almost out of thin air over the last twenty years, is worth more than three times as much as all the gold extracted by all the miners during the entire California Gold Rush.

The online marketing world is the new gold fields, where anyone can supposedly strike it rich. And it's not just the providers of online platforms and tools that are hitting the motherlode. There are stories of everything from office workers quitting their jobs to make a living by following their real passion for cooking with a blog about recipes[4] to Internet-based retailers spiking sales by

---

4 https://www.youtube.com/watch?v=XU7TDLMJjnM

targeting specific demographics online[5] to organic farmers growing their business a hundredfold through Google search advertising.[6]

The stories of success and transformation flow constantly. It truly does seem like a time when you can get something for almost nothing. It's a mentality that online marketing pitchmen—which represent some of the very companies that have already struck it rich—continue to promote. No doubt, all the "hype" and promotion around online marketing has an effect.

THE ILLUSORY TRUTH EFFECT

In 1977, a researcher at Villanova University conducted an experiment[7] to prove that the more times people hear something, the more they believe it's true—whether it is or not. Sixty study participants were given a series of statements to review. Some of the statements were true, some were untrue and some were vague. Participants were asked to rate whether they felt each statement was true on a scale of 1 to 7 with 7 being absolutely true and 1 being absolutely false.

The participants came back every two weeks for three sessions and rated sixty more statements. Twenty of those statements were the same through all three sessions. No matter whether the statements were true, false, or vague in reality, each time the participants saw the statement an additional time, their rating of whether it was true or not increased. The average score for those twenty repeated statements on the 7-point scale was 4.2 in the first session, 4.6 in the second session, and 4.7 in the last session.

There were no other patterns in the results. The scores went up for all the statements that were shown more than once regardless

---

5 https://www.facebook.com/business/success/smartbuyglasses
6 https://www.youtube.com/watch?v=6i4nU-x0xJ8
7 https://en.wikipedia.org/wiki/Illusory_truth_effect

of whether they were really true or not. This means that a person is just as likely to believe a false statement as a true statement if they hear (or see or read) it repeatedly.

This phenomenon is common in today's world. Politicians are able to convince their constituents of things by repeating talking points, no matter how outlandish, over and over again. "Fake news" spreads across the Internet and gains credibility the more it's shared, despite being proven to be completely fabricated.

In the Villanova study, the "illusory truth effect" could be seen after a person was exposed to a statement only three times. Today's business owners probably hear from pitchmen and media outlets that "everyone is doing online marketing these days" multiple times per week–hundreds (maybe thousands) of times per year. It's no wonder that, over time, owners come to believe that online marketing is an imperative for their business.

THE PROOF IS IN THE PALM OF YOUR HAND

The dream of easy riches is just as powerful today as it was for prospectors a hundred and fifty years ago, but there is something that makes the gold fever of today potentially even *more* alluring than it was for those miners of yesteryear: we carry around a tangible reminder of it in our own pockets.

8

MACHINE MASTERS

"We become what we behold. We shape our tools,
and thereafter our tools shape us."

~ Marshall McLuhan (1911–1980), Canadian professor,
philosopher, and media theorist

Something dramatic happened to our species at a magical moment forty thousand years ago—an event that relates to the problems we have with online marketing today. After billions of years of Earth's history and millions of years of human evolution, all of a sudden, human beings began drawing and writing on the walls of caves. Not just one cave in one location, but drawings on cave walls in all the corners of the globe by people with no contact with one another.

In the Cave of El Castillo in Cantabria, Northern Spain, scientists have dated a red ocher disk that's associated with extensive cave drawings to at least 40,800 years ago.

At virtually the same moment on the opposite side of the world, inhabitants of the tropical island of Sulawesi in Indonesia began decorating the walls of Pettakere Cave with their own art.

The ages of the cave drawings in Spain and Indonesia are so close that each claims to be the oldest in the world. Experts disagree about which one wins the crown, but one thing seems certain: both cultures began creating very similar cave art independently at the same point in history. Some spark was lit in humanity and from that moment on, paintings and rock art exploded all over the world, from Europe to Africa and Asia and even in the Americas among populations with no contact with the rest of the world.

And that red ocher disk discovered in El Castillo? It was one of the first pieces of communication technology ever used by man—a prehistoric ancestor of Facebook, if you will. Forty millennia later, we're still posting our messages on a "wall" for the world to see.

THE TOOLS OF COMMUNICATION

Since our prehistoric ancestors created those first cave drawings, the tools that humans have used to communicate with one another have developed in two areas: the technological tools to record and transmit a message from one person to another, and the artistic and symbolic tools to help the recipients of messages understand what the sender intended.

Those early hand paintings at Pettakere and El Castillo are examples of successful transmission of a message (after all, it has traveled intact to us forty thousand years after it was "sent"), but a failure in terms of us understanding what the sender was trying to communicate. We can only guess at the purpose and meaning of those drawings.

Over time, however, humans began to develop ways to communicate concepts more clearly, first with pictograms (images that literally look like what they are trying to communicate) and then ideograms (images that convey an idea or concept beyond their literal form). These two communication forms were very effective for simple messages, and they are still used commonly today in signage and advertising. Pictograms and ideograms also allowed early people to put combinations of images together to tell stories.

Finally, a few thousand years ago (3600 B.C. in Samaria and 600 B.C. in Mesoamerica), a huge leap took place with the invention of written symbols that were tied to spoken language. All modern spoken languages have a written counterpart, usually composed of an alphabet, organizational structure, and punctuation—like the English used in this book.

Pictogram with the meaning of "dog" and ideogram communicating "no dogs allowed"

We are so accustomed to this system that we don't give it a second thought, but written language dramatically increased our ability to communicate with one another as a species because it has two very interesting characteristics.

First, written language is an incredible lever that allows us to do a lot of work with very little effort. It's elegantly simple while simultaneously possessing almost infinite power.

Rather than needing to have a pictogram to represent every item and idea in the universe, a few symbols could be configured into an almost infinite variety of meanings. In English, there are twenty-six letters and a few extra characters for punctuation. With only those few symbols, we can express any idea we can imagine. The Oxford English Dictionary contains almost 250,000 words[8]—all built from the same twenty-six characters. Imagine if you had to memorize 250,000 different pictograms in order to understand English! And, of course, we can arrange those words in millions of different combinations, giving us the ability to communicate anything we can conceive of.

Second, written language is also a set of instructions. The symbols we use to build words each have a corresponding spoken sound. We all know how to make a specific sound when we see the letter *d*, for example. We are so comfortable using written language in our everyday lives that we never stop to realize that a word like "dog" communicates more than just the idea of man's best friend. It also communicates how to form vocal and verbal sounds to say the word out loud. This means that written language is actually a way of transmitting *sound*.

With all of the video and audio transmitting and recording devices that exist in our modern world, we think nothing of seeing or hearing someone else speak on the radio, TV, or YouTube. But imagine a world without electronic recordings. An ancient Roman citizen living on the edges of the empire would have been able to hear the actual words of Caesar in their heads and even speak those words themselves thanks to written language—not just the general idea, but the actual words. More than two hundred years after they were first written down, we ourselves can both "hear" and speak Thomas Jefferson's immortal words from the Declaration of Independence ("We hold these truths to be self-evident, that all men are created equal . . .") as though we were actually there at the Continental Congress in 1776.

---

8 https://en.oxforddictionaries.com/explore/how-many-words-are-there-in-the-english-language

Written language, then, was the first invention to allow our spoken human language to be recorded, transmitted, and reconstructed accurately across space and time. If you've ever read anything aloud to fellow classmates or an audience, you've used both aspects of written language at the same time: receiving and comprehending the information from the writer while disseminating it to others by following the phonetic instructions encoded in the symbols.

Along with these amazing advances in the symbolic systems of written communication, humans also continued to develop the technological recording and transmission devices to store and send those messages from one person to another. Clay tablets, palm leaves, wax tablets, and papyrus were paired with brushes, styli, lead pencils, and many forms of pen and ink.

By about two thousand years ago, human communication technology and symbolic systems had developed to the point that some of the most important and lasting works ever created by humanity began to emerge. The combination of pen, ink, and written symbols gave birth to nearly all of the foundational religious texts that guide the world today. Chalk, chalkboard, and mathematical symbols were all that was necessary to communicate the most profound laws of our physical universe. Philosophers, artists, and lovers were able to communicate ideas and emotions so powerfully that words written hundreds or thousands of years ago by someone we've never met can cause us to laugh or weep still today. A few symbols on paper still perfectly transmit pain, love, and wonder directly to us from Greek playwrights like Sophocles across twenty-five centuries of time and space.

The improvements in written communication over the last forty thousand years truly rank as one of the most important advances in human history.

Then, computers arrived.

TOOL TYRANNY

Throughout history, advances in the technology of creating, storing, and transmitting a message or idea from one person to another (or from one person to many people) were driven by a desire to communicate more deeply, richly, and effectively. Innovations as diverse as calligraphy, color printing, and television were all attempts to deliver a message from one person to another with ever more intellectual and emotional impact. Communication technology's role was subordinate to the message itself.

But beginning about ten years ago, technology took over in a cultural coup. We have fallen so in love with the technology we use to communicate with one another that we are letting it dramatically impact what we're able to say and how we're able to interact. More and more, our interpersonal interactions are limited by technology (as opposed to being enhanced by it), and we've become okay with that. Accurate spelling and standard grammar usage are in decline. We've gone from typing with ten fingers to typing with two thumbs. Our language (that rich, symbolic communication system we've worked to develop for forty thousand years) has been reduced to acronyms and emoticons that will fit onto a miniature screen—because, of course, you have to say everything in 140 characters or less. Today, the technology of creating, transmitting, and storing ideas, concepts, and emotions has become more important than the message itself. It's no surprise when you consider how our brains react while we're using technology.

THIS IS YOUR BRAIN ON FACEBOOK

Business owners, like just about everyone in society these days, are addicted to computers and smartphones. And like anything that's addictive, making clear and rational decisions about how and whether to use it can become clouded by that appeal.

The digital and social media world is one of constant action. Email and text messages arrive around the clock. Social media feeds have new posts from friends and companies in a never-ending stream. And if things that are delivered to you aren't enough, there is a bottomless supply of video and web content to seek out and consume.

This continuous flow of stimuli causes measurable changes in our bodies every time we consume it: our heart rates slow, brain blood vessels dilate, and blood flows away from major muscles. In fact, researchers have shown that these physiological reactions are so powerful that they happen even when we just *anticipate* looking at the stream of media available on our computers and smartphones. These responses involve the neurotransmitter dopamine, a brain messenger that modulates all sorts of activities involving reward, feeling good, and exploration. It's an unconscious reaction that makes us all respond to what psychologists call a "seductive psychological draw" exactly the same as any other potentially addictive activity or substance from shopping to cocaine.[9]

One of the aspects of modern technology that's so appealing to our brains is the amount of content available for us to consume—an unlimited supply of stimuli. This shouldn't be a surprise since the role of automation and technology is to increase the efficiency and

---

9 https://www.psychologytoday.com/blog/brain-bootcamp/200907/techno-addicts

quantity of output. Advances in farming technology increase yields, factory automation reduces production costs, computer improvements allow for faster computations, and communication technology increases the ease with which we can interact with thousands or even millions of other people. But more is not always better.

Compared to the heartfelt handwritten love letters of the Victorian era or even the hours and hours spent on the phone by teenagers years ago, we've become a quantity-over-quality society with no depth thanks to the mile-wide, inch-deep nature of the technologies we've become so reliant on.

Now technology isn't only affecting how we communicate, it's affecting how we initiate and nurture entire relationships.

THE RISE OF THE TECHNOLOGICAL RELATIONSHIP

On the surface, the idea seems so appealing: You map out an ideal business relationship and create a series of automated messages and interactions that will walk a prospect through the stages of first contact, acquaintance, rapport-building, and so on... leading eventually to them becoming a customer.

The idea is appealing because it promises that the tool will do all the work. In reality, though, the relationships aren't deep and the automation fails because of its inauthenticity. Humans are socially savvy creatures tuned over millions of years of evolution to spot fraud and dishonesty. We all have a "disingenuous sense" that tells us when someone approaches us in a manner that's only in their own best interest.

I love asking CEOs who are sending out automated email drip campaigns to open their own inbox and show me a message they've received from someone else that they themselves responded to. They suddenly realize the fallacy of thinking that something that doesn't work on them will magically work on others. They have fallen prey to the twisted logic of loving the technology and forgetting that sales and marketing is really about making a human connection.

The bottom line is that no matter how much we all love technology, it cannot by itself build a relationship with another person. Real relationships still require a human.

THE DEVIL INSIDE

This phenomenon, where business owners recognize (and are turned off by) everyone else's self-serving, computerized marketing messages while at the same time thinking that their own self-serving messages are really resonating with people out there, is something that has fascinated me over the past few years. The erosion of ethics in our society, get-rich-quick gold fever, and our love affair with technology are powerful forces, but is there more going on? Is there something else that's keeping business owners from recognizing the obvious absurdity of the snake oil pitch they've been sold?

It turns out that there *is* another culprit lurking in the shadows—possibly the most powerful culprit of all: our own brains.

9

FLAWED FEEDBACK

"I've learned that people will forget what you said, people will forget what you did, but people will never forget how you made them feel."

~ Maya Angelou (1928–2014), American author and poet

Pyrrhus of Epirus, a Mediterranean leader who lived around 300 B.C. was once considered one of the greatest military commanders of all time. The great Carthaginian leader Hannibal even compared Pyrrhus to Alexander the Great.

His most famous victory was against the Romans in 280 B.C. At that time, Rome was a growing power and the states around it were fighting back against Roman expansion. The southern Italian city of Tarentum (at the top of the "heel" of the boot-shaped Italian peninsula) was a Greek city threatened by Rome. The Tarentines asked Pyrrhus to lead an army against the Romans on their behalf.

Pyrrhus arrived in Italy with a formidable force of over twenty thousand men, three thousand cavalry, and fifty war elephants (something the Roman soldiers had never faced before). He took on the Romans at the Battle of Asculum and while both sides suffered heavy casualties, Pyrrhus was able to win the day. His victory at Asculum, however, exposed an underlying weakness in his situation.

The Romans were fighting in their own backyard and could easily bring up more men to replace the ones they lost. Pyrrhus was on foreign soil, far from home. He could not replace men, animals, and equipment lost in battle as easily as the Romans could. Even if he won every battle, he would eventually be doomed as his army was slowly weakened. The Romans could

Bust of Pyrrhus of Epirus

win the war by attrition as Pyrrhus's forces were slowly reduced in strength even as he was winning battle after battle. In fact, Pyrrhus is said to have famously remarked after one successful fight, "If we are victorious in one more battle with the Romans, we shall be utterly ruined."

Pyrrhus was eventually forced to retreat from his Roman campaign despite his string of battlefield victories, and we remember him today for the term "Pyrrhic victory," a phrase that describes a small victory that's, in reality, a defeat in the big picture. Pyrrhus is also the inspiration for the concept of winning the battle while losing the war.

ONLY PART OF THE PICTURE

Successes or failures in today's marketing world don't have the same grand, historical implications of sweeping battles between ancient empires, of course. But the same pattern of small victories leading to a big-picture defeat plays out every day for businesses who have fallen for the online marketing pitch. They are often on a path to ruin that's just as certain as the defeat that Pyrrhus faced—they just can't see it as clearly as he could.

Pyrrhus was beside his men as they fought and fell on the battlefield, and he could appreciate firsthand that he could not afford to continue his string of "victories." He was face to face with the reality of his situation. In our modern, digitally-connected world, however, business owners face a paradox that clouds their judgment of whether their small victories are leading them to eventual success or failure: they're not actually "on the battlefield." It's as if they are fighting battles by remote control.

On one hand, we are connected with more people than ever before thanks to the power of computers and online networks. At the same time, those computers and networks keep us physically isolated from the very people we're interacting with. This is true in our personal lives and as well as in the world of online marketing.

We might see someone post something funny on Facebook, but we aren't actually in the same room with them to share the laugh. We can send someone a message of congratulations, but we can't be there to look them in the eye and shake their hand. We are able to share condolences, but we can't give someone a hug.

In both our personal and business lives, rather than having deep, meaningful interactions with a few people, we have shallow, transient interactions with hundreds or thousands of people. Very little (and definitely not *enough*) information actually flows back and forth between people in modern electronic channels. It's like we're trying to have relationships through the keyhole of a locked door rather than being in the room with the people we're interacting with.

Here is a simple example: my friend Tom sent me a text the other day and I answered with something I thought was funny. Tom replied to my funny line with "LOL," a response we've all received many times. On the surface, we all know that the acronym "LOL" stands for "laughing out loud." But was Tom *really* laughing out loud? Maybe it wasn't funny to him at all and he was being polite because he didn't want to hurt my feelings. Maybe he thought it was worth a smile but not literally laughing out loud and he just didn't have an acronym or emoticon for "smiling but not laughing out loud" handy to send to me.

The point is that there is no way I could actually know for sure. The three characters of "LOL" that Tom sent through the keyhole were not enough information for me to know exactly how he felt about my message.

What happens next is where the danger lies, because our brains are wired to helpfully fill in the gaps when we don't have enough information on an important issue. It's a tendency that can lead us to erroneous conclusions.

MIND THE GAP

Since Tom is my friend and his feelings about me are important to me, my brain makes it a top priority to collect and analyze as much information as possible to let me know if my interaction with Tom was successful or not. Since I interacted with Tom through a digital keyhole, there is very little information (only three characters) available that's actually from him.

So what does my brain do? It fills in the gaps with other information that it *does* have access to: my own thoughts and feelings. If I thought that my line was only a groan-worthy pun, I'd interpret his "LOL" as a wry smirk. If I thought the message I sent was a gut buster, I would interpret his "LOL" as though he literally did laugh out loud spontaneously to the point where people around him (wherever he was) might ask what was so funny. Without sufficiently rich feedback from Tom himself, my brain more or less assumes he felt the way I intended for him to feel—which means that my brain categorizes the interaction as a success. Scientists call this tendency of our brain to see what it was hoping for—especially when faced with limited or ambiguous evidence—as confirmation bias.

The danger of confirmation bias, of course, is that I could be completely wrong. I could believe Tom thought it was hilarious while he was actually thinking it was terrible. And I could keep misreading Tom's responses, interpreting them as I desired, continuing down a path that might even harm our relationship—all the while, thinking that I was nurturing it.

We all see this play out in various ways in our digital lives. On the harmless end of the spectrum, there are people who love to send or post humorous emails or social media messages to acquaintances. All it takes is a few "LOL's" from people on their distribution list for them to continue excitedly sending more of them indefinitely, believing that everyone thinks the messages are as entertaining as they do. On the other end of the spectrum, the harmful end, extreme behaviors like cyber-stalking and bullying can result.

LESS THAN LOL

Businesses who have fallen for the online marketing pitch are also susceptible to confirmation bias. They could be believing that they are nurturing relationships while in reality they are damaging them. Plus, businesses using online marketing have a challenge that's even larger than the one I had with my friend Tom.

At least I got three characters of response back from Tom. It isn't much, but it's something. Most of the time, businesses following the advice of online marketing pitchmen have even less than that to go on. They are interpreting their progress in a relationship by things as small as the opening of an email or a click of a mouse. This is akin to me trying to interpret Tom's response to my funny text by knowing only that he opened it. Tom's three character "LOL" reply to me—that originally seemed so limited—seems like a *huge* amount of information when compared to what businesses are dealing with in online marketing.

FEEDING THE BIAS

Confirmation bias is something we all deal with in our lives, but online marketing pitchmen exploit it. They talk about clicks and opens and downloads only in positive terms. They create reports for businesses that interpret stats on those behaviors as good results. The pitchmen never tell business owners that those clicks or opens or downloads could be harming the relationships they are trying to nurture. But in the real world we see that this is often the case.

I have clicked on ads that made me angry when I realized they were misleading. I've opened emails that seemed to be addressed just to me only to find they were spam. I've downloaded ebooks only to find that they were sales pitches posing as helpful content—feeling as if I was tricked into giving my contact information in return for something of little or no value.

We have all had this experience.

The senders of those communications, however, thought they

were nurturing relationships when all the while they were actually harming them. They interpreted our clicks and opens and downloads as positive events because of their natural inclination toward confirmation bias and the eternally sunny reporting provided by the online marketing pitchmen to make the business owners think that they were succeeding.

This disconnect is one of the reasons that so many business owners I talk to are confused about why their online marketing isn't producing the results they expected (acquiring new customers and increasing revenues) even though it appears to be performing well in all of the reports they see.

They are winning lots of small "battles" by getting people to open emails or click on ads, but unlike Pyrrhus, they are so biased that they don't even realize that while they're winning the battles, they're losing the war.

BUT WAIT, THERE'S MORE

The way our brains play tricks on us with confirmation bias and the way that online marketing pitchmen take advantage of the situation is bad enough. Unfortunately, though, there are other areas in which the pitchmen use our brains against us.

It turns out that there are several ways that online marketing, helped along by the pitchmen, can be addictive.

10

HEAD GAMES

"If you stop at general math, you're only going to make general math money."

~ Calvin Cordozar "Snoop Dogg" Broadus Jr. (b. 1971),
American rap music artist and actor

The human brain is wired to look for patterns. It's a powerful ability that we use subconsciously and automatically. We evolved this capability as a species to help us survive in a very competitive and dangerous world. Remembering a pattern that occurred previously when we found a food source helped us to recognize that scenario again. Likewise, noticing the characteristics of a hazardous situation helped us to avoid that peril down the road. The better we were at recognizing patterns, the more successfully we could compete and survive.

Unfortunately, our subconscious desire to find patterns is often more powerful than our intellectual ability to truly assess whether those patterns are real or just an illusion.

There are industries that take advantage of the fact that customers are prone to seeing patterns that don't actually exist. They happily profit from the biases built into our brains that lead us to make poor decisions when presented with large amounts of random data. One of the most obvious of these is the casino industry.

There is only one reason that casinos have a digital readout next to every roulette table showing the numbers that have come up over the most recent rolls. They know that those past rolls have absolutely no impact on what will happen on future rolls, but they also know that customers will see patterns on the board and come to believe they can predict what is likely to happen next. This encourages customers to put their money down and take a chance.

The casino purposely provides customers with data that it knows is meaningless (albeit presented as "helpful" information) expressly to trick the brains of customers into gambling more. And casinos are not alone in this practice. The pitchmen of online marketing do exactly the same thing to encourage businesses to spend more and more time and money on online marketing.

DASHBOARD DANGERS

Akin to the readout next to the roulette table, the device that online marketing pitchmen use to lure business owners into spending more is the "dashboard." All of the large online marketing platform companies like Google and Facebook, as well as the tool providers like HubSpot and Constant Contact, have built-in reporting—commonly called dashboards in the marketing industry.

But just like the casino that provides "helpful" information next to the roulette wheel (and in myriad other forms throughout the casino), online marketing pitchmen know that much of the data in customer dashboards serves only one purpose: to get the business to keep spending more and more on online marketing.

In fact, both casinos and online marketing pitchmen know that the "helpful" data they provide is so engrossing that it's actually addictive, trapping unsuspecting customers in a self-destructive cycle.

There are, in fact, three beliefs and behaviors that I see in business owners who continue to invest in online marketing even when it's apparent that it isn't working—beliefs and behaviors that are also commonly seen in compulsive gamblers.

I SEE THE PATTERN

The human brain tries to find meaningful patterns within random data, a phenomenon scientists call apophenia. It happens all the time in casinos: red has come up six times in a row so it seems like black is more likely to come up next; craps players get on a lucky streak after changing the way they hold the dice before tossing them, and now they believe they've found a way to improve their odds; or someone playing blackjack feels like he always loses more when a certain dealer is at his table. Online marketing pitchmen take advantage of apophenia by providing large amounts of data and presenting it as though it's important and relevant. Google Analytics alone has more than one hundred built-in reports that feverishly display official-looking percentages and pie charts, whether the information is useful or not. Usually, the data is not important at all (it's just random fluctuations or simple correlations), but marketers and business owners often fall into the trap of trying to find important patterns within it: "Last week's blog article has attracted traffic from Russia for some reason," or "Why has our sharing rate trended up for three straight months?" or "We put the word 'hello' in our email subject line and now our open rate is down." Apophenia associated with the flood of unimportant data from online marketing programs causes business owners who would otherwise recognize that online marketing doesn't work to instead believe there are hidden answers that they just haven't unlocked yet. Consequently, they stick with an online marketing approach long after they should have bailed on it.

I'VE GOT A SYSTEM

It's no coincidence that "action" is a synonym for gambling. Gamblers tend to feel as if they have an active role to play in the outcome of their wager—even for games that require no skill whatsoever like roulette, slots, or lotteries. A gambler will frequently take action based on the patterns they think they are seeing as the game progresses, believing that they are actually having an effect on the results. This is called the "illusion of control," and casinos go out of their way to feed on this by providing gamblers with all kinds of tactical decisions to make in the course of most games: which numbers to pick, how much to wager, whether and by how much to increase the bet if the likelihood of winning improves as the hand progresses, and so on. These decisions give gamblers the illusion that they are somehow in control of the outcome. Even in completely random lotteries, players are likely to believe that their own choice of specific numbers will have some bearing on their chances of winning. In online marketing, there are even more tactical decisions to make: what content to use, how much to spend on an ad, or which keywords to use, just to name a few. These tactical decisions lead business owners to believe that they play a more significant role in the outcome of the campaign than they really do. If a campaign fails, there is a tendency to then personalize the failure and assume that it was because of their own faulty decision-making. There are always more ways to try different tactics (a different subject line, a more specific keyword, an infographic instead of text). Rather than considering the possibility that online marketing, in general, just doesn't work for their business, the owner and their marketing team end up trapped in an endless cycle of tactical iteration, attempting to achieve the success they believe is sure to come if they can just get the recipe right.

I'M GETTING BETTER AT THIS

A third way that our brains fail us in gambling situations is through what researchers call the near-miss response. For a physical task like shooting a basketball free throw, our brain gives us a positive feeling if we get closer to making it than if we're way off—and that positive feeling prompts us to try again. On the scorecard, a miss is a miss if it doesn't go in—no matter how close we get—but we *feel* better about ourselves and know that we're getting closer to making it if the ball *almost* goes in. Gamblers feel the same rush when they've almost won a bet—even in games of complete random chance. Four numbers matching on the lottery out of eight? We're halfway to winning the prize! Two cherries out of three on the slot machine? We're getting closer to a big payoff! Of course, in games of chance, getting close on this roll of the dice has no relevance to what will happen on the next roll, but researchers have found with MRI scans that our pleasure centers light up as much on near misses as they do on actual wins. It's our brain believing that we're getting better (like we would be if we were getting closer to the basket on each free throw attempt) and encouraging us to keep going toward our goal. As with gambling, online marketing dashboards, with their continual flood of tactical (and often, useless) information, provide many opportunities for near misses. Click rates commonly jump around due to sample sizes that are too small to be used for important decision-making, but business owners think they're getting closer to knowing what combination of advertising words will bring in loads of traffic. Or the business gets listed at the top of a Google search ranking for one keyword but it moves down in the rankings for another, making business owners and their marketing team feel as if they are closer to having a reliable process for getting to the top of the listings. Or a social media post goes viral, encouraging the business owner to keep at it to try to repeat that viral effect again and again. Like a mirage that's always just out of reach, business owners continue to strive for online marketing success even when they shouldn't. The false feeling of progress they get from those supposed near misses is that strong!

BREAKING THE CYCLE

I've sat with business owners many times and looked at the results of online marketing programs that clearly aren't working. The dashboards show marketing metrics—such as traffic, opens, clicks, and followers—that look positive but the campaigns are not resulting in revenue.

Time and again, however, the owners and their managers continue to persist in the belief that digital and social marketing is imperative for the future success of their business. They've been brainwashed by the barrage of propaganda from the pitchmen and are afraid of being left behind. Getting them to realize they've been brainwashed is often akin to an intervention.

When I am finally able to break through, the next step is to rebuild their sales and marketing efforts from the ground up based on four principles that will help them get (and stay) on track in the face of all the hype that will keep coming at them.

PART 3

....

CORRECTING

How to see past the hype and confidently chart
your own path for marketing and business success
in the modern digital world.

11

DEFINING THE DESTINATION

"If you don't know where you're going, you'll end up someplace else."

~ Lawrence "Yogi" Berra (1925–2015),
Hall of Fame baseball player and humorist

Pitchmen are like the mythical Sirens in the ancient Greek story *The Odyssey* by Homer, who sang beautiful songs of false promises that lured passing sailors from their planned route onto the rocks of destruction. In *The Odyssey,* the hero of the story, Odysseus, had his men plug their ears with beeswax so that they could not be distracted by the songs of the Sirens. This allowed the ship to avoid the trap and safely keep to its true course.

The siren song of the pitchmen is that there is a better way—a magical new way—that seems too good to be true. Like a magic pill that helps you lose weight while you sleep or a perpetual motion machine that generates more energy than it consumes, the pitchmen promise that new clients and revenue will appear in your email inbox each morning thanks to a few simple keywords, website tweaks or downloadable ebooks. It sounds so attractive. But in the end, it's just a false promise.

The first step toward getting back on the right track is coming to the realization that you have been following the advice of self-serving pitchmen. Then it's time to chart a new path: one that's authentic to the values of your business and effective in realizing your goals. The first step in laying out that new path is to clearly articulate the desired destination.

MIND YOUR OWN BEESWAX

Just as Odysseus plugged the ears of his men to keep them from falling for the songs of the Sirens, business owners who have fallen for the promises of the online marketing pitchmen need a way to ignore the false claims in order to stay on (and in some cases, get back on) their true course. They need to develop a "pitch-proof" focus and a business mindset that is permanently immune to slick-sounding marketing gimmicks and fads.

The way to do that is to clearly document what the true course is for your business. Where is the business going? What was the origin of the business? How did it get from where it began to where it is today? How can the business grow and achieve its goals for the future?

The answers are different for every business. There is no one-size-fits-all solution to growing a business (contrary to what the pitchmen will say). But there is a process any business can undertake to lay out a course that's right for its particular goals. It starts with defining the desired destination of the business. The good news is that most business owners have been there before, so the past is the key to success in the future.

BEST OF THE BEST

Consider your best customers: who are they? How did you win their business? How have you served them over the years? Don't default to "speaking in profiles," i.e., "Our best customers are companies in X industry that are Y size and have Z problem." Online marketing pitchmen train business owners to think this way because they are in the business of selling high volumes of activity aimed at anonymous lists of targets.

Instead of describing profiles of business types, focus on *individual* businesses. Name three specific companies that you have as customers currently or have had in the past that you would consider to be the best customers you've ever had.

Undoubtedly, your business would love to have more Best Customers like this—with a sales and marketing program that results in more of these ideal customers going forward. Remember Odysseus: make sure that those Best Customers are representative of the ideal "destination" for your business.

Next, explore what it is that makes (or made) those customers the best. The answers are not the same for every business owner, but the definition of a Best Customer usually includes some combination of characteristics from four categories.

Financial considerations are usually the first that come up. Best Customers often represent higher revenue and/or higher profits. Predictable future revenue and profitability due to long term commitments or contracts is also a common attribute of a Best Customer.

Beyond such financial characteristics, a variety of operational and cultural traits define what sets exceptional customers apart from the rest of the pack. In many industries, a business must integrate its operations with the systems, processes, and tools of its customers, and vice versa. Customers where that operational integration happens most seamlessly are often cited as the best type of customers. Cultural attributes also come into play when describing the Best Customers. Honesty, transparency, integrity, and a collaborative win-win approach to problem solving are frequently cited as important traits for Best Customers to possess.

Sometimes Best Customers are ones who help a business get even more customers. Such a customer might actively refer other potential customers to the business, act as a passionate reference when called upon, or simply bring a level of prestige to the business ("Oh, you're working with them? Impressive!"). But in any case, business owners tend to value more highly those customers that help bring in more customers.

There are also a variety of relational attributes that can define a Best Customer. Business owners value customers who have been with the company a long time and those who took a risk by hiring their business early in its life. Business owners also talk about situations where customers are really valuing and benefiting from the work the business does (as opposed to a customer who is buying the product or service but not really using it to its fullest). A business owner who is passionate about what they do often relishes the customers who are equally passionate about the service their business provides.

The thing I find interesting about the ways in which business owners describe their Best Customers is that the majority of what they talk about is how their businesses interact and interface with those customers. Sure, money is significant, but it's not the only thing that matters. I've never had a business owner describe a Best Customer as one who spends a lot of money but is difficult to work with or sees no value in what the business provides. Those kinds of customers definitely exist, but they are never described as the kinds of customers the business owner wants more of. Financial considerations are important, but they aren't all that matters when it comes to the kinds of customers many businesses are after. There are a set of subjective qualities that make some customers the Best and others not. Even the closest of competitors who go head-to-head in the same industry will end up with different sets of criteria for what each of their Best Customers look like.

Ultimately, based on both financial and non-financial considerations, the roster of your business's Best Customers emerges. The objective is to paint a portrait of what your ideal customer looks like, and assuming your business wants more customers like those Best ones, the portrait you've painted can serve as a template for what the goals of your marketing and sales effort of your business should be—a vision of the "destination" your business is striving toward.

This "defining the destination" process is the first step toward making a business pitch-proof when approached by a snake oil salesman with a new fad or gimmick. Like a guiding star, it can be kept in view to make sure that the business stays on course.

Of course, just having a destination clearly defined doesn't tell a business exactly which route to take to get there. Knowing where your business wants to end up doesn't guarantee that, along the way, the Sirens won't lure you onto the rocks by promising that there is a shortcut or better way to achieve your business goals.

Therefore, in addition to knowing your destination, you must also map out the route that will safely and reliably get you there. Luckily, since you've been to your desired destination already, you have charted the path to get there. You don't have to follow a plan proposed by a pitchman with a self-serving agenda. Your business need only follow in its own footsteps.

12

THE ROOT CAUSE OF SUCCESS

"It is important for us to understand where we came from and how we got here because it would be very foolish of us to get off that horse we rode in on."

~ Bruce Nordstrom (b. 1933), philanthropist and former chairman, Nordstrom, Inc.

Knowing where your business wants to end up in its sales and marketing efforts by clearly articulating the destination in terms of what an ideal client looks like is a good start. But as we all know from using the mapping apps on our smartphones, you can't plan a route to a desired destination without knowing where you're starting from.

To get more of those Best Customers described in Chapter 11, go back and discover where those best-of-the-bests came from. How did you first meet them? How did they hear about your business (and vice versa)? What steps did the relationships go through before they became Best Customers? How long did those various steps take?

In a sense, what you need to do is conduct a type of root-cause analysis to dig back to the very beginning—uncovering the original events that eventually led to today's Best Customers.

One of my favorite root-cause analysis techniques was developed over a century ago by the owner of a small loom manufacturing company in Japan. In the late 1800s, Sakichi Toyoda's Automatic Loom Works made weaving machines for textile manufacturers, and some of the ideas that he came up with for his loom manufacturing company went on to affect the world well beyond the textile industry.

For example, Toyoda innovated by adding the idea of *jikoda* into his machines: the ability for a machine to detect that it's malfunctioning and automatically shut itself down to avoid causing more damage to itself or the rest of the manufacturing process connected to it. In the era of the Model T automobile, the idea that a machine could "know" that it was having a problem and take action to prevent further problems was truly ahead of its time.

Sakichi Toyoda

Sakichi Toyoda's manufacturing innovations, in fact, were so successful he became known as "the father of the Japanese industrial revolution," and his textile loom manufacturing company continued to grow, expanding to manufacture many other modern types of equipment and machinery—eventually becoming today's global conglomerate Toyota Industries.

In addition to creating new ways for machines to manage themselves, Toyoda was also a genius at innovating ways for the people in his company to work together more effectively and efficiently.

5 WHYS

Sakichi Toyoda's machines might have been able to stop themselves when they developed a problem, but decades before the invention of the computer, those machines were definitely not capable of knowing why something had gone wrong. That required a human.

Toyoda also realized that it was important to get past the obvious problem and drill down to find the root cause of whatever had gone wrong. If a belt broke on a machine, it wasn't enough to simply replace the belt and move on. It was important to also figure out why the belt broke to see if broken belts could be permanently eliminated as a future problem.

The approach that Sakichi Toyoda developed over a century ago—still in use as part of today's Toyota Production System—was called 5 Whys. The idea was that engineers would drill down at least five levels into a problem (asking "Why did X happen?" getting the answer, "Because of Y," and then asking "Okay, then why did Y happen?" iteratively five times) to make sure they had gotten to the real core of the issue. This approach allows Toyota teams to find solutions in innovative places that have led to dramatic improvements in mechanical as well as human systems and processes.

BACK TO SQUARE ONE

Business owners who are frustrated and confused with the program they've been sold by online marketing pitchmen benefit from a root-cause analysis approach similar to Sakichi Toyoda's 5 Whys process. Consider the Best Customers you've identified and drill down five levels to explore what originally led to those companies becoming customers in the first place.

For each Best Customer, move backward through the chain of events that culminated in the great relationship your business has with that customer today. Go back to the first contract, the original proposal, and the first meetings, even to the earliest interactions between people in the two companies.

As you delve into the past, is there something that you keep finding when you have identified the origin of these Best Customers? Indeed, when I do this exercise with my clients there is often a single person who can be identified as the original wellspring that the entire subsequent business relationship grew from. Along the way, several people might have been involved in various aspects of the interactions between the business and customer, but when we trace everything back to the very beginning, we usually find there was one person who started it all. We call those people Critical Business Relationships (CBRs).

CBRs come in many forms. They might be an outside, third-party advisor who knew of a problem that a business (let's call it Buyer, Inc.), was having and suggested that another firm they knew of (yours) might have a solution. A CBR might even be the owner of Buyer, Inc., who knew you or some key member(s) of your team from some other walk of life (Rotary, church, a nonprofit board, and so on). They might be an influential employee at Buyer, Inc., who had worked with your business in some capacity at some point in the past. Or, they could be a current or former customer of yours who endorsed your business to the decision makers at Buyer, Inc.

No matter what their specific role and no matter whether they were inside or outside of Buyer, Inc., the universal trait of CBRs is that they were willing to lead the way in facilitating a potential business relationship between your business and Buyer, Inc.

Not only do CBRs play a special role in bringing you together with Buyer, Inc., they are relatively rare—and therefore, very valuable. Some companies have grown by millions (even hundreds of millions) of dollars from only a handful of CBRs.

Unfortunately, in today's fast-paced, electronically connected world, the idea of finding and nurturing valuable long-term business relationships is often seen as old-fashioned. There is a common belief in the business world these days that scaling up a business means finding ways to computerize and automate things. Anything that's human-centric is viewed as inefficient and an impediment to growth. And it's not just the online marketing pitchmen who have this viewpoint. Just about any time I have a discussion with any consultant, professional investor or business analyst about business growth, a common theme that comes up is efficiencies that can be realized by replacing humans with computers throughout the business: on the factory floor, administering employee benefits, and even answering the phone.

The online marketing pitchmen play off this attitude by selling the idea of reducing or even eliminating the human-centric aspects of marketing and sales. They promise a world where the "old-fashioned" organic, person-to-person relationships that established trust and credibility are replaced by the perfect keyword, blog post, or email newsletter. It sounds alluring, but the absurdity of this belief is exhibited regularly in my inbox.

In today's world, of course, everyone is bombarded with unsolicited emails and newsletters every day. At least once a week, I get one that has some variation on the same message: "We treat every customer as one of a kind." The company sending out the message (let's call them "Vendor Corp.") usually goes on to share how everyone else in their industry treats customers like an anonymous number, but at Vendor Corp. they will know my name and give me the personal attention I deserve. They also frequently explain their trademarked assessment or evaluation process that will help them customize their Vendor Corp. solutions to my specific needs. Lastly, they always implore me to only select a potential vendor who will treat me as individually as they will.

I continue to be amazed that companies that send messages like this can't see that they are making the most compelling case ever for not choosing them. Somehow, they are blind to the ridiculous contradiction of sending out a mass, unsolicited, impersonal email that talks about how they treat every potential customer individually.

It's obvious to me in these situations that companies like Vendor Corp. understand that they have to develop trusting relationships with potential customers—they've just been convinced by the online marketing pitchmen that they can build that trust and rapport en masse without having to actually engage with those potential customers personally.

IF I HAD A HAMMER

In his 1966 book *The Psychology of Science,* Abraham Maslow, the American psychologist who developed the famous Maslow's Hierarchy of Needs, included the concept "if all you have is a hammer, everything looks like a nail."

The online pitchmen are convinced that their hammer is the solution to every sales and marketing challenge. Their message is so seductive that they are able to persuade business owners that concepts like trust and reliability are just keywords that can be used to lure potential customers in—as opposed to being attributes that are earned through actions over time.

The pitchmen never say, "You know, it looks like key individual relationships have been pivotal in the way you've built your business—maybe an impersonal, automated approach isn't best for you." They never say that because, well, they only have a hammer so all they see are nails. The pitchmen don't see that there could be a way to scale up a business predictably and systematically using the digital tools of the Internet and social media age we live in without abandoning the "old-fashioned" idea of building real, long-term, *individual* human relationships.

Fortunately, such an approach does exist.

13

THE MISSING MODEL

"The computer can't tell you the emotional story. It can give you the exact mathematical design, but what's missing is the eyebrows."

~ Frank Zappa (1940–1993), American musician, composer, and filmmaker

The ways in which business owners can use online tools and techniques to grow their companies are almost countless. From search engine optimization to pay-per-click to email marketing to webinars to viral videos to a thousand other options, it can be overwhelming to try to make sense of it all.

Ultimately, however, all of those options can be grouped into four distinct marketing models. And by looking at each model from a big-picture perspective, business owners can quickly see which model (or combination of models) is most and least likely to be successful for their particular business.

KEYING ON KEYWORDS

The most well-known of the four online marketing models is Inbound.

The premise of the Inbound model is that potential customers are out there looking for the solution you provide and you just have to make sure they find and select your business to fulfill their need. The goal of Inbound marketing is to appear (and look enticing) in the results on Google, Bing, YouTube, or other search engines when the prospective customer performs a search. Search engine optimization (SEO) is the practice of working to get your website to come up in search results when prospective customers input particular words or phrases into the search engine that may indicate they are in the market for what your business offers.

SEO tactics include adjustments to the behind-the-scenes coding of your website, which allows the search engine's algorithms to more easily "read" what your site is selling. Posting high volumes of new content to your website (usually in the form of blog articles) that are rich in the keywords that potential customers might input is another tactic that can encourage the search engine algorithms to select and display your site over others.

One of the challenges of SEO is that success (getting to the top of the search results) is a technical exercise of trying to make your site appealing to algorithms instead of making it appealing to humans. It's an esoteric exercise that can be very complicated and frustrating.

Rather than trying to get your site to be displayed in the search results that come up when a prospective customer types in a term that's on target for what you sell, there is another option you can pursue: pay Google or Bing (or YouTube, Yahoo, or any search engine) to put an advertisement on the page next to those search results. This paid version of search engine optimization is called search engine marketing (SEM) and, in theory, it requires less fiddling with website code or keyword-rich content. Just pay the money and voilà, there you are on the first page. Of course, there are thousands (or millions) of companies clamoring to get onto that page ahead of you, so the search engine companies have set up an auction system where paying the most gets you the slot. This means that SEM can become an expensive proposition. But if the right search terms are available at an affordable price, it's an approach that can be successful, especially for consumer-focused businesses that are selling a simple product or service.

The major limitation of the Inbound model is that it only works if potential customers are searching for what you offer. If you are selling books or shoes or hotel rooms, it could work for your business. But buyers of more complicated and customized products and services like corporate legal services, custom software integration, or factory automation equipment aren't surfing around looking for a new supplier in Google search results.

As attractive as the concept of the Inbound model is, there are a lot of businesses for which it just isn't a good fit.

GETTING VIRULENT

After Inbound, the second most well-known marketing approach is the Viral model.

Viral marketing is most often associated with social media. The idea is that you post something interesting to your connections and they like it so much, they share it with their connections and then those people share it with their connections, and so on. This sharing can create a chain reaction where your original post spreads to thousands or even millions of people in an exponential explosion.

Getting content to spread virally is very attractive, because it can generate a huge amount of exposure at little cost. Offsetting the potential cost savings, however, is the fact that it's exceptionally hard to reliably create content that *will* spread virally. When I talk to business owners about the Viral model, I tell them that it's like nitroglycerin: incredibly powerful but equally unpredictable.

For business owners who want to use the Viral model to scale up their sales, there are two additional challenges:

1. **It'll Cost Ya.** Over the last few years, social media platforms like Facebook and LinkedIn have noticed that viral content made lots of money for whomever was able to hit on something catchy. Those social media companies have moved to cash in on potential viral content on their sites. They do this by limiting the number and kinds of people your post will reach, then charge you to "boost" the post so that more people will actually see it. This means that you actually have to pay to get your own posts to all of your own followers—and that's before it has a chance to start spreading from person to person.

2. **It's Showtime.** One of the biggest impediments to taking advantage of the Viral model is that, in many cases, it doesn't fit the personality of the owner or that of their company. Viral content is dramatic content. It typically must be brash or shocking or over the top in some manner to cut through the noise of our busy lives and attract attention. For business owners wanting to project values of integrity, trust, and reliability, becoming a brash showman looking for the spotlight often isn't a good fit.

The unpredictable nature of the Viral model means that it's a difficult approach to take by itself to build a business, and the "look at me" nature of the content necessary to succeed with the Viral model is not a fit for many businesses. At best, it's usually a secondary tactic in a larger marketing approach.

IT TAKES A COMMUNITY

The third approach that business owners typically think of related to online marketing is the Community model. In the Community model, people gather to interact around a shared interest.

Users of particular products, whether those are consumer or business products, often form communities to share their ideas and experiences. Harley-Davidson motorcycle owners interact with one another extensively and will strike up a conversation with other owners anywhere, anytime. Users of various types of software also often form groups to discuss and share successes and challenges they've had using that software.

The hallmark of any community, however, is that members of the community are more attracted to other members of the group than they are to the company that provides the product or service they have in common. A Harley owner is excited to talk to another Harley owner—as excited (or even more so) than they would be to talk with someone from the Harley-Davidson company itself.

Online, there's an array of places where like-minded people come together in communities, from social media channels such as Facebook to dedicated websites to LinkedIn Groups.

For business owners who would like to build their sales and marketing strategy to be based on a community model, there is one key question that must be answered: do the users of your product or service want to talk to *each other* about it? If the answer is not a very strong yes, a Community model is unlikely to succeed.

There are several common dynamics that can inhibit or preclude the development of a vibrant Community:

- **No Time.** It takes time to participate in a group, and many potential Community members just don't have enough time to get engaged, even if they wanted to.

- **Secrecy.** Sometimes, the users of a particular product or service don't want the world to know what they are using behind the scenes for competitive reasons. As a result, potential Community members can be reluctant to publicly discuss anything of significance. This is very common, for example, in LinkedIn groups. The vast majority of LinkedIn Group members sign up to gather intelligence from what other members are saying while never sharing anything themselves (the term for this behavior is "lurking").

- **Image.** The best sharing within any Community occurs when a member shares a challenge they are having. But this requires that a particular member show vulnerability, which can be very hard to do in a business setting. It's one thing for a Harley owner to post a question about which brand of spark plugs to use when doing a tune-up, but it's quite another for a corporate executive to post a question that indicates they don't know about some important aspect of their job.

For businesses with products and services that lend themselves to the formation of a customer or industry Community, the model can be a very powerful one. Unfortunately, in my work I've seen many businesses invest significant resources in an attempt to form Communities without ever achieving success.

THE MISSING MODEL

The Inbound, Viral, and Community models are the options that are most well-known (and talked about) in marketing circles. There is a fourth model, however, that many business owners don't consider when they think of online marketing: the 1-to-1 model.

The 1-to-1 model is just as the name implies: treating people as individuals, interacting with each person one at a time. It's a model that's not typically associated with online marketing because it can't be automated, but it's one of the most powerful. It's a model that aligns perfectly with businesses that have an owner or sales team with a focus on building personal, individual relationships with potential customers. (Typically, these are businesses with long selling cycles and large, complex sales.)

In Chapter 12, I showed you the power of Critical Business Relationships (CBRs) as a driver of growth for many businesses. The 1-to-1 model aligns perfectly with the CBR idea—it helps build and nurture those valuable relationships. The 1-to-1 model doesn't align well, however, with what the online marketing pitchmen want to sell, because the pitchmen are usually focused on volume.

The pitchmen are typically rewarded for quantity over quality, so rather than help a business deepen relationships with the CBRs that will actually drive growth, pitchmen convince the business owner that high volume SEO or content marketing or email blasts will work instead.

And speaking of email blasts, there are pitchmen who will try to make the case that email marketing is 1-to-1 because, while thousands of messages are sent out at a time, emails are delivered to each recipient individually—and the email can even have the recipient's name in the salutation. The 1-to-1 model, however, is about *interacting* with a person as an individual, not just delivering messages to them individually. It's about messages going back and forth in order to have a meaningful two-way conversation.

The difference seems subtle until you consider a quick, real-world example. Imagine that you are at the opening networking event at a convention and you are walking around mingling with other attendees. In the true 1-to-1 model, you spend time chatting with various people, asking how their flight was, inquiring about how their business is going, and catching up on what's been happening in their life since you saw them last year. You each share stories and a few laughs. Now, let's pretend we're following the email blast approach that the pitchmen will say is "1-to-1." You would walk quickly from person to person and say a predetermined speech about what's been going on with you in the last year. Then you'd pause for a few seconds to see if they said anything (which none of them would because, as statistics show, recipients of email blasts might open them, but they never *reply*). With no response, you'd flit off to another person and try your speech again. Yes, you would be delivering your preplanned speech to one person at a time, but you would not be engaging in individualized 1-to-1 *interactions*.

The pitchmen know all this, of course, because even though they don't tell business owners to engage in the 1-to-1 model, they use it extensively for themselves.

DO WHAT I SELL, NOT WHAT I DO

It's hard to go to any business networking meeting or conference without running into reps and consultants peddling online marketing snake oil. They are everywhere—and they're there *in person*. At the local level, there are thousands of small agencies and solopreneurs swarming around every gathering of business owners touting online marketing or some related software product as a panacea. The giant national players such as Facebook, LinkedIn, and Google have their own sales reps (put $50 into LinkedIn ads and your phone will ring within minutes with a call from a helpful LinkedIn rep who will assist you in finding ways to spend even more), and they partner with "certified" local agencies and consultants to give themselves more in-person representation all across the country. Almost every business owner I've ever talked to who purchased online marketing bought it from a sales rep in an in-person, 1-to-1 sales pitch.

Some of the pitchmen recognize that what they themselves do is not what they're recommending to customers, but some are in a major state of denial. I was talking with a vice president at one of those local digital marketing agencies recently and this person proudly told me that they have more than eighty local reps on the streets proactively building relationships in the community and "helping spread the word about the power of online marketing." Amazingly, the vice president didn't see the irony in that statement.

As an industry, though, the online marketing pitchmen know that 1-to-1, relationship-based selling is an important part of how they grow their own businesses. They just neglect to help their clients do the same thing.

What all this means is that business owners have to choose the models that are right for their own business and not blindly rely on pitchmen to provide a biased recommendation. For most businesses, there is a combination of models that is appropriate, but the bottom line is that if the 1-to-1 model is an important component (which it probably is if CBRs are valuable in driving growth), the business owners themselves will need to push to ensure that 1-to-1 is part of their marketing strategy.

ALL SYSTEMS GO

One of the challenges that business owners sometimes run into when thinking about building individual relationships is that they do it so intuitively that they don't think about doing it *systematically*. Most of the important relationships they have are probably ones that have developed organically over time, and the business owner may not have been explicitly thinking of nurturing those relationships as part of a formal process.

But if 1-to-1 relationship building is to be used as a purposeful, predictable part of a business growth plan, it can't be left to random chance. A process is necessary. This doesn't mean that the relationships are not authentic. A process just means that you'll make sure you don't let other tactical things in life distract you from keeping up with the relationships that are important to the success of the business. It also means always remembering exactly how relationships are built over time.

14

HOW RELATIONSHIPS WORK

"Companies in the East put a lot more emphasis on human relationships, while those from the West focus on the product and the bottom line. Western businesspeople often don't get the importance of establishing human relationships."

~ Daniel Goleman (b. 1946), psychologist and author of the bestseller *Emotional Intelligence*

The starting point for developing a process to initiate and grow Critical Business Relationships (CBRs) is to define the universe of relationships that are possible. For any new relationship to form between you and another person, three conditions must exist. First, the person must be the kind of individual you want to have a relationship with. Second, that person must be open to meeting someone new. And finally, you must have (or be able to build) enough rapport with that person in order for the relationship to start and subsequently flourish.

Most important, only two of these three criteria are under your control. You have the ability to choose (and adjust) the kinds of people you want to have a relationship with. You can change your ability to build rapport, but you cannot control whether other people are open to meeting anyone new. This is a mistake that business owners who have fallen for the stories of the online marketing pitchmen make regularly. The business owner believes that just because they have found someone they want to have a relationship with, they can simply convince that person to have a relationship with them. They believe that persistence or even coercion can actually change that person's desire to engage in a relationship.

The Universe of Potential Relationships

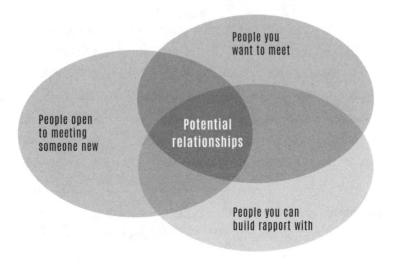

That's not to say that people don't change their behavior. A person who doesn't want to meet anyone new now may want to in the future. But if they are not open right now, attempting to force the situation creates a negative experience that may preclude you from ever having a relationship with them. The love-struck "stalker," the "won't take no for an answer" telemarketer, and the company that repeatedly sends unsolicited email with no way to opt out are examples of continuing to try to push someone to have a relationship with you even when they don't want to... and likely ensures that you *never will* have a relationship with them.

If you attempt to initiate a new relationship with a CBR and they indicate they are not interested in meeting anyone new (or they just ignore your outreach), put them into a "try again later" category and wait a while before reaching out to them again. Also, check to see if you've done the best job you could have at actually forging a relationship with them. It's possible that they're open to meeting someone new, but that you just didn't present yourself to them in a way that struck a chord.

FINDING COMMON GROUND

Once you've identified someone you'd like to meet (who is also open to meeting you), or someone you already know with whom you'd like to deepen your relationship, the way to build a relationship with that person is to identify things you have in common. The strongest human bonds are not formed when two people like each other. Rather, the strongest relationships form when two people both like the same thing. Those "same things" that people share are called commonalities. Commonalities can be anything from a similar sense of humor to a shared love of wine to having the same alma mater. Commonalities provide the basis for interactions with another person—they literally are the "relate" part of the relationship. Having (or finding) things that you have in common with another person is the way to strengthen any human relationship—in your personal life or your business life.

Many times, we find commonalities with people randomly or even accidentally. That's how most people find their friends or significant others—through a bit of luck. But it's possible to set about finding commonalities purposely in order to build better relationships with CBRs. There are an almost unlimited number of potential commonalities to choose from, falling into five general types:

- **Characteristics.** This is about what and who you are. Title/responsibilities, industry certifications, age/gender, ethnicity, group memberships, physical traits, and family situation are examples of potential shared characteristics.

- **Behaviors.** What you do and how you do it can also be a potential source of bonding. Being very organized or disorganized, following the rules or breaking them, being boisterous or quiet: people who have similar behaviors are more likely to form a relationship than those who don't.

- **Experiences.** This is related to where you've been and what you've done in the past or what you are going through right now. Travel experiences, raising kids, working at a certain company or job, living in a particular place, or going through some sort of life event are examples of potential shared experiences.

- **Interests.** Here it's about what you enjoy. The list of potential shared interests is long: hobbies, sports teams, movies, music, food, vacation destinations, particular authors, business gurus, sunny weather . . . the list goes on and on. Interests provide the widest variety of potential commonalities of all.

- **Opinions.** This is about what you think and how you see the world. Political views, religious affiliation, commentary on current events, and business industry views fall into this category. Opinions are the most volatile of all commonality areas: they can forge incredibly strong bonds between people, but they can also alienate people who don't share your opinions, so care must be taken to ensure that your opinion is one that the would-be CBR agrees with.

Using all the possibilities within those five commonality types, we could take any two completely random people in the world and, within a few minutes, uncover a healthy list of commonalities between them. This means that enough commonalities exist to allow you to potentially form a relationship with anyone in the world, including, of course, the people you'd like as CBRs. All that's required is an opportunity to communicate what you share with them—and the right techniques to use when you get that opportunity.

BUILDING RAPPORT

Knowing the commonalities you share with a CBR is the raw material for a relationship. To refine that raw material into an actual relationship, there is a series of rapport-building techniques to use when you have the chance to interact with the CBR about the things you have in common with them, including:

- **Mirroring.** Generally, you want to try to match the style and formality of those you're communicating with. In person, it's something most of us do naturally. Handshakes are a good example. There are many different kinds of handshakes, from the formal palm grip to slightly more casual variations that include an exaggerated outreach motion or additional hand touch to even more familiar varieties that incorporate alternative hand grips and hugs. Figuring out which type is appropriate in any given situation is something most people are at least fairly good at. When a handshake is imminent, our brains use a combination of factors: what is generally appropriate to the social setting we're in, visual clues about the personality of the person we're greeting, what our history is with that person, and even behavioral clues from the other person as we approach them. We usually get a handshake right. The same goes for the conversation that follows the handshake. In person, we're usually pretty good. But many of us aren't as good at mirroring in digital communications. With a little thought and practice, however, we can be. It's just a matter of stopping to think about the other person and how they seem to like to interact digitally. Do they use full sentences or short phrases? Do they use acronyms and shorthand or spell everything out? Do they stick to the topic at hand or add in other comments? Do they respond during the business day or after hours? Do they have a formal signature or just their initials at the end of their message? Attempting to mirror the style of a CBR as much as is feasible is always a good way to subtly let that person know you're relating to them.

- **Going First.** The strongest relationships are those where people give before receiving. Finding ways to do something nice (even if it's simply mentioning that you're thinking of them) without asking or expecting anything in return shows your CBR that you care about them as a person and not just as someone you want something from.

- **Asking Questions.** Usually, people respond well to being asked about something they have some interest, expertise, or experience in. This doesn't mean you should create a question that's a thinly veiled sales pitch (i.e., "Hey Jack, do you have a problem getting enough sales?"). Rather, use questions to develop a personal relationship with the CBR beyond the business relationship you are desiring. Find some other commonalities to ask about.

- **Pacing.** Relationships tend to have an appropriate cadence for interactions. In general, new relationships start more slowly and build over time. Established relationships can go through different phases where there is more or less interaction at different times. It's important to determine a communication frequency that's appropriate to the relationship and, when in doubt, space communications out a little longer. When the goal is forming or deepening a relationship, too much communication is worse than too little.

- **Minimizing Business.** If your CBRs know what you do and what products and services you offer, you should rarely, if ever, talk about your business. Even if the relationship exists in a business environment (i.e., you see the CBR mostly at business events, such as networking or industry gatherings versus seeing them in other settings like kids' soccer games, the golf course, or Rotary meetings), we usually recommend that less than 10 percent of communications be related to your business.

- **Maintaining Consistency.** As in the tortoise and hare fable, slow and steady wins the race. Staying engaged with the CBR over the long run indicates loyalty and caring on your part. It's important to show that you value them as a person even when there is no imminent business to be done together.

- **Remembering Them.** Finding a way to refer back to previous interactions in communications is a powerful way to signal that the recipient is important to you. Examples include inside jokes, reminders of funny shared moments, remembering (and commenting) on something important that they said previously, and so on.

- **Being Responsive.** It's ironic that in a time when technological tools enable us all to have a higher volume of communications than ever before, so many people (and businesses) don't respond when reached out to. You can stand out by being responsive. Even if it takes a while, a delayed response is better than no response at all. Responses are also a great chance to utilize other techniques, such as mirroring and remembering.

By choosing potential CBRs who are open to having a relationship, finding commonalities with them and using the techniques of rapport building, it's possible to put a systematic program in place to nurture CBRs that will bring in a steady stream of Best Customers, regardless of which of the four marketing models you employ.

There are many excellent modern digital and online tools available to help in the execution of a CBR nurturing program. And the fun part is that many of the tools are the same ones that the online marketing pitchmen have been convincing businesses to use—it's just that with the CBR program in mind, those tools can be used in ways that benefit your business, not the pitchmen.

15

TOOL SCHOOL

"It's not the tools that you have faith in–tools are just tools. They work,
or they don't work. It's people you have faith in or not."

~ Steve Jobs (1955–2011), American businessman,
inventor, and industrial designer

In general terms, there are two opposing forces at work when
you look at the products and services that are available in the online
marketing world: efficiency and effectiveness. The pitchmen tend
to line up on the efficiency side of the equation. They make more
money when there is more volume of activity (either by selling
advertisements on the pages that people visit or by selling higher
subscription levels to reach more people), so they try to encourage
businesses to get more followers, more opens, more clicks, more
"likes," and to send more messages. They do this by making it really
easy to send the same message to thousands of people at once and

by reducing interactions to a single click ("click here to congratulate Bill on his work anniversary") or less ("click here to automatically send Bill a congratulatory note on his work anniversary every year"). But by definition, if you're sending the same message to multiple people or to the same people multiple times, you're not treating that person as an individual—you're certainly not showing the recipient that you understand or care about them as a person.

When I receive those generic email or social media messages, where people just clicked a box or the send button to congratulate me on a birthday or anniversary, I often think of the old Hallmark Cards slogan, "When you care enough to send the very best." However, I imagine it as "Wow, they cared enough about me to send the very *least*." It tells me where I rank in their lives—and it definitely does not build rapport with me.

Still, it's easy and quick and it's what the pitchmen say you should do when that feature pops up. But efficiency is not effectiveness. Effectiveness in a two-way relationship requires that you treat each person as an individual.

Thankfully, there are as many tools available to help with the goal of effectiveness as there are on the dreaded efficiency side of the equation. In some cases, they are exactly the same tool—just used in a different way.

THE FIRST PLACE TO LOOK

Twenty-five years ago, I spent several years in a sales position where I traveled a lot to visit potential customers. There were many things that salesmen like me did in those days that are a lot less common today. For example, I remember just dropping in on prospects unannounced to say hello. They were always quick visits where I would stop in at the front desk to ask if the owner or manager was in (I'd ask for them by name) and if they had a minute for me to say hello. Often, they'd come out to the front desk and we'd have a quick chat for a couple of minutes. Sometimes they'd invite me to come back to their office for a longer visit.

When we got back to their office, the first thing I'd do as I walked in would be to scan the desk and walls for photos and plaques. It's a standard rapport-building technique of old-school, in-person salesmen to look for conversation starters among the things a prospective client has put on display. Charity golf outing photo? Family portrait? Awards? All of those things provide clues about what the prospective customer likes. Since, of course, you build a relationship with another person by liking what they like, my goal was to find something on display that I could strike up a conversation about. Even if I didn't know anything about golf, I could at least ask questions about the photo (where it was taken, how they got into the sport, when the last time was they were able to get away for a good trip, etc.). It's Sales 101. With more sales and marketing being done electronically by phone and email these days, though, fewer sales reps have the chance to visit (and scan the walls of) a prospective customer's office in person. But the good news is that there are many ways to accomplish the same thing with online tools.

The obvious first place to look when sizing up the interests and passions of a potential customer is their own social media accounts, followed by online searches for articles and/or press releases from or about them.

Like the photos and plaques on office walls, those accounts and search results will show what the prospect is into—from charities they support to where they went to school to where they've worked in the past to who their friends and families are.

In many ways, it's even easier to learn what a potential customer likes today than it was years ago before the Internet age. Back then, I had to get invited back to their office to see what they cared most about. Now their "office photos" are visible to the entire world on the web. There really is no excuse in our modern world for not being able to find some commonality with any potential customer.

BIONIC HEARING

In the 1970s science fiction TV series *The Bionic Woman,* main character Jaime Sommers has several mechanical and electronic enhancements made to her body after a skydiving accident. One of those was a bionic ear that allowed her to hear things that were too quiet or distant for normal people to hear. With her enhanced hearing, Jaime could isolate and listen in on conversations between bad guys from as far away as two miles away as though she were right next to them. This allowed her to succeed in many covert spy missions. But the Bionic Woman's abilities are nothing compared to the ability we all have to hear what other people are saying in the modern world.

In social media, conversations play out live in real time—often for the whole world to see. Using the golf example from my old traveling salesman days, I was able to see that my potential customer enjoyed golf, because of the picture on their wall, but today we can all see that potential customer on their golfing trip in real time as they post photos of the trip on social media.

And even when the potential customer is reclusive and shares very little of their personal life online, it's still possible to hear conversations they care about. They may not post things about their alma mater, but the school itself will talk about its new stadium or latest championship. The prospect may not post online about their spouse or kids, but it's likely that those family members are active in their own right. And they may not make a big deal about the charity they support, but that charity will promote the fact that it's having its annual fundraiser.

The Bionic Woman was able to hear the conversations of two people from miles away, but the ability to "listen" using the Internet today is like being able to hear the conversations of all of the people and organizations your potential customers knows. It's a power that would make Jaime Sommers jealous—and again, it means that there's no excuse for not knowing what's happening in the life of your potential customer.

IF MEMORY SERVES ME CORRECTLY

Greek mythology contains hundreds of gods and other immortals. One of my favorites is Mnemosyne (pronounced *neh-MAW-sen-ee*). We get our modern word "mnemonics" from Mnemosyne, the goddess of memory.

What I like most about Mnemosyne is that not only was she the goddess of memory, she was also the mother of the Muses, the nine goddesses of creative inspiration in literature, science, and the arts. In this way, the Greeks represented memory literally as the source of all creativity.

Painting of the goddess Mnemosyne

The idea that memory leads to creativity is especially appropriate when thinking about how modern tools can help us build rapport with Critical Business Relationships. In fact, there are two ways that having a better "memory" can help us do a better job at initiating and building important relationships:

- **Remembering the Past.** In Chapter 14, we talked about how referring back to things that have happened in the past in any relationship helps to maintain and build rapport with that person. In today's world, we usually have a complete record of the exchanges we've had with people. They are recorded and available for recall in detail in many ways: CRM software systems can store communications we've had with people, social media platforms keep track of messages sent through them, and even the "sent items" and "received items" folders in our email and text programs hold copies of previous interactions that we can call up on demand. Without too much effort, it's possible in today's digital world to always refer to some previous event or topic whenever we create a new message to the people we want to nurture a relationship with.

- **Remembering the Future.** Not only can we have 100 percent recall of what has happened in the past, modern tools can also ensure that we'll never forget to reach out to our important CBRs in the future. It's easy to schedule a regular cadence of interactions and reminders in our CRM systems and other common tools, such as Outlook, that we use every day. With today's tools literally at our fingertips, it's easier to purposely stay "on the radar" of people you'd like to initiate or deepen a relationship with like never before.

EFFICIENT EFFECTIVENESS

At the beginning of this chapter, I talked about there being a trade-off between efficiency and effectiveness in the online marketing world. Focusing on efficiency for its own sake (as the pitchmen recommend) leads to mass, automated messaging that's impersonal and destructive to relationships. But efficiency doesn't have to be a bad thing—as long as we make sure that we don't sacrifice effectiveness to achieve it.

When you start with an unwavering commitment to effectiveness by treating the important relationships in your business life like they really *are* important (finding commonalities with them and using rapport-building techniques), you can safely use digital tools to become more efficient. This will allow your business to manage and nurture as many CBRs as possible.

There is no denying the fact that we live in a technologically dependent world. Indeed, technology has the power to make us more productive than ever before. We just have to continually ensure that those tools serve us instead of the other way around.

EPILOGUE

....

THE TWAIN SUMMARY

"Wisdom begins at the end."
~ Daniel Webster (1782–1852), early-American lawyer and statesman

One of the first questions that authors face when thinking of writing a book is whether they have enough material to fill up an entire book. It's one thing to have an idea that you want to share with the world; it's quite another to flesh that idea out and make it interesting for thirty or forty thousand words. Some of the greatest writers in history, however, have recognized that longer is not always better. Getting a

Mark Twain

point across in shorter fashion is always preferable to taking the long route to the final destination.

There is a famous quote that's often attributed to Mark Twain from a note he supposedly wrote to a friend that sums up the idea perfectly: "Please excuse my lengthiness; if I'd had more time, I'd have written a shorter letter."

It turns out that Twain never said exactly those words, but he did express the sentiment many times. A number of famous writers and storytellers throughout history have also expressed the virtue of taking the time to edit a story down to its most succinct form, from the ancient Roman philosopher Cicero to Benjamin Franklin to, of course, Mr. Twain.

As I've researched and written the entertaining historical stories of Clark Stanley and Montgomery Ward and Pyrrhus of Epirus for this book over the last several months, I've also had an enjoyable little side project: working to see if I could distill the concept of this book into the *shortest* form possible. I've called this side project the "Twain Summary."

I believe I've gotten the Twain Summary of *Clicksand* distilled down to three symbols:

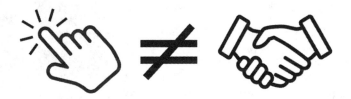

Originally, the Twain Summary idea was just an entertaining way for me to open up my mind and think differently about things as I wrote the book, but once it took shape, I realized it was also the perfect way to end.

If every business owner simply kept those three symbols top of mind as they make decisions about how to market their business, fewer businesses would fall prey to the false promises of online marketing pitchmen—and more owners would remember that authentic, individual relationships are what drive success for most businesses.

It's your choice: the thirty-thousand-word version or the three-symbol version. Whichever option works best for you, here's hoping that you can avoid the clicksand trap and reach the goals you have for your business.

TAKING ACTION

"Do or do not. There is no try."

~ Yoda, from "Star Wars: Episode V - The Empire Strikes Back" (1980)

If you're this far into *Clicksand,* it's likely that the ideas I've been discussing have struck a chord with you. If that's the case, I'm thrilled. That in and of itself is a victory. Sometimes, just having a heightened awareness of what is happening around us is enough to cause a change in behavior. I've had many readers tell me how they can recognize the pitchmen of online marketing, and that they're making different decisions in their businesses because of what they've read in *Clicksand.*

Other business owners, however, wonder if they might be caught in the trap without fully realizing it. After all, every business owner has to use email and social media these days, and they have to have a website that they hope potential customers will visit. And, most business owners are getting advice from outside advisors about how to use those tools. So how can a business owner know if they have unwittingly strayed (or been led) into the clicksand trap? In the Prologue, I discussed the five emotions that owners trapped in clicksand tend to feel: frustration, confusion, fear, dissonance, and isolation. If you, as a business owner, are experiencing any (or all) of those feelings, it is a good indication that your business might be in danger.

To help, here is a short quiz to help you gauge whether or not you are caught in clicksand.

DO YOU HAVE A SINKING FEELING?

For each of the five questions below, circle the number that best represents where you, as a business owner, fall:

A. If you've tried it, what results have you gotten from online marketing?

1 • 2 • 3 • 4 • 5 • 6 • 7 • 8 • 9 • 10

We've gotten more than we could have hoped for   We've seen absolutely no results from it

B. How knowledgeable do you feel you are personally about online marketing?

1 • 2 • 3 • 4 • 5 • 6 • 7 • 8 • 9 • 10

I totally understand how it all works   I have no clue about any of this stuff

C. Do you feel like you're behind your competition in the use of online marketing?

1 • 2 • 3 • 4 • 5 • 6 • 7 • 8 • 9 • 10

We're ahead of everyone else   Everyone else seems to be way ahead of us

D. Do the online marketing techniques you're using match your company's values?

1 • 2 • 3 • 4 • 5 • 6 • 7 • 8 • 9 • 10

It's a great fit with our values   We're doing things that are not a fit with our values

E. Do you feel the people around you see something about online marketing that you're missing?

1 • 2 • 3 • 4 • 5 • 6 • 7 • 8 • 9 • 10

No, I'm aligned with everyone else   Yes, everyone seems to "get" it but me

After answering all five questions above, add up your scores and see if you're caught in the clicksand trap:

10 or less	11-20	21-30	31 or more
All Clear	**Be Careful**	**Warning**	**Danger**

GETTING ADDITIONAL HELP FOR YOUR BUSINESS

Many businesses that are caught in the clicksand trap are able to free themselves by returning to what made them successful before they were lured in by the online marketing pitchmen. They're able to rekindle their relationship-building culture and processes and get back on track on their own.

Others, however, need a little more than just a book; they need assistance getting their sales and marketing effort onto the right path. Sometimes, those businesses have a relationship-oriented past that got them to a certain level, but they don't know how to build a repeatable, predictable system around relationships in order to keep growing. Other times, a business has no history of investing in long-term business relationships and no idea it is even possible.

For those businesses that need help, the team at Civilis Marketing can provide several services designed to get everything going in the right direction:

- **Discovery.** Who is really important to your success? Following Sakichi Toyoda's 5 Whys approach, Civilis does an historical analysis to figure out which relationships are most valuable and why. Then they'll help you make a plan to initiate and deepen your relationships with the very people who are most important to your success.

- **Design**. Using the relationship-development techniques described in Chapter 14, Civilis designs a customized relationship-building program that includes relationship goals, message types, program cadence, metrics and reporting.

- **Execution**. A great plan is useless if it sits on the shelf gathering dust. The relationship-building experts at Civilis actually nurture your important relationships (for you and as you) day in and day out. They make sure your business maintains the consistent relationship-building momentum that pays off over the long haul.

If your business needs help getting out of the clicksand trap, connect with Civilis Marketing online at www.civilismarketing.com or by email at info@civilismarketing.com.

FURTHER DISCUSSION

Lastly, if you'd like to share and/or explore the concepts you've read in *Clicksand* in more depth with me, visit www.clicksand.net to:

- Have me speak at your corporate or industry event as a keynote speaker.
- Book me for an interview on your radio, TV, or podcast show.
- Get more clicksand stories and inspiration from my blog.
- Share your own clicksand story with me.

....

ACKNOWLEDGMENTS

"At times our own light goes out and is rekindled by a spark from another person. Each of us has cause to think with deep gratitude of those who have lighted the flame within us."

~ Albert Schweitzer (1875-1965), theologian, physician, philosopher, humanitarian, and musician

There are some creative exercises, like painting or sculpting, that come to fruition from a single artist's inspiration and energy. Then there are those creative endeavors that are team efforts. Movies, TV shows, and theater productions, for example, are the cumulative result of an army of different specialists. I'd always had the impression that writing a book is one of those single artist ventures. But through the process of writing *Clicksand* I've learned that while the author might have the idea for what they want to say, bringing that idea to life in book form requires the help of an army of friends and professionals.

The first phase of support for an author comes from the people who made a difference before a single word of the book was ever written. In my case, that includes my mom Lucy Rovang (for passing on those rebellious Bullard family genes and for teaching me the value of examining the contrarian point of view) and my dad Hal Troy (for giving me the gift of persistence to keep at it until the job is done—and done well). It also includes my brother Matt, who has been a kindred "contrarian+persistence" spirit in life.

Hugh Cathey, Ross Youngs, Kurt Hanson, Reg Johns, Tim Medland, Janie Kirkland, Terry Bettis, Steve Larson, Rob Sherwood, and Joe Geoffroy were all instrumental in giving me opportunities and guidance as mentors at various points in my career and I owe them all a big debt of gratitude for arriving at the place where I could contemplate a project like this.

Special thanks to Jonathan Little, who has had a profound effect on me over the twenty amazing years we've spent together at TroyResearch. And thanks to his wife, Betty, for putting up with the business adventures that Jonathan and I have cooked up over those two decades.

There were many valuable people who played roles in the creation of *Clicksand* and they deserve credit for their contribution:

- Rex Elliott and Chip Cooper for listening to me rant about what was happening in the marketing industry and being among the first to say the world needed to hear the *Clicksand* message.

- Cary Hanosek, Frank Agin, and Don DePerro for being the living embodiments of relationship-oriented professionals.

- Jim Young, Michael Fisk, and Scott Humphrys, who gamely waded through early versions of the *Clicksand* manuscript and offered very helpful (and needed) suggestions for improvement.

- Fellow Entrepreneurs' Organization member authors Mark Moses, John Ruhlin, Kevin Stoller, Sandy Fekete and Lisa Cini for sharing their own experiences so candidly in true "EO style."

- Leyl "Master" Black and her music list from dEOxidized that provided the soundtrack to my most productive writing sessions.

- The eternally energetic and amazing Deb Gabor for selflessly sharing everything as she traveled the road ahead of me.

- Longtime friends Scott Wilson and Tripp Eldredge for, respectively, thirty years and countless miles questioning assumptions.

I have also been struck by the publishing industry professionals who have been willing to help with *Clicksand* for the good of the project—and sometimes even against their own self-interest. These people have been an inspiration and deserve my gratitude:

- Glenn McMahan of Endeavor Literary Services for advice and developmental editing on my earliest drafts.

- Sandy Smith of Smith Publicity for selfless guidance on navigating the publishing industry.

- Rohit Bhargava of IdeaPress Publishing for being a contrarian after my own heart.

- Terry Deal for making me sound like me, only better.

- Marnie McMahon for keeping the trains running on time.

- Alban Fischer for making *Clicksand* beautiful outside and Jessica Angerstein for making it beautiful inside.

Lastly, it's a fact of life that a book is just entertainment if it doesn't translate into real change in the world. I am grateful every day for Kim Troy, Allison Greene, and the entire Civilis Marketing team for taking the ideas from this book and turning them into practical tools and services that help businesses get out of the clicksand trap.

And speaking of my wife Kim, much of the credit for this book goes to her. She has been inspiring me to be a better version of myself ever since we first met in Regester Hall as college freshmen at the University of Puget Sound too many years ago. She is the power source that drives all of my creativity and accomplishments.

INDEX